CREATING A
SUCCESSFUL
Retirement

CREATING A
SUCCESSFUL
Retirement

Finding Peace & Purpose

RICHARD P. JOHNSON, PH.D.

Liguori
LIGUORI, MISSOURI

Published by Liguori Publications
Liguori, Missouri 63057

To order, call 800-325-9521, or visit liguori.org

Library of Congress Cataloging-in-Publication Data

Johnson, Richard P.
    Creating a successful retirement : finding peace and purpose / Richard P. Johnson
        p.   cm.
    Includes bibliographical references and index.
    ISBN 978-0-7648-0497-7
    1. Retirement. 2. Retirees—Psychology. 3. Retirees—Conduct of life.
I. Title.
HQ1062.J64   1999
646.7'9—dc21   99–37631

Liguori Publications, a nonprofit corporation, is an apostolate of the Redemptorists. To learn more about the Redemptorists, visit Redemptorists.com.

Printed in the United States of America
11 10 / 9 8 7

Contents

Introduction

*"Retirement is a spiritual journey every bit as much as it
is a financial, emotional, and psychological one."*

R. P. JOHNSON

This book is a manual on how to make your retirement
the most satisfying, fulfilling, and personally captivat-
ing time of your life. After more than twenty-five years
as a retirement counselor, I've discovered fifteen "pearls" of
retirement wisdom that spell the difference between success and
failure in retirement—whatever you conceive retirement to be.
These fifteen pearls are solid principles that anyone can put into
productive action. Each one serves as a rung on a ladder leading
to retirement life success.

This is a practical book that offers specific answers; it's also
a spiritual book because it speaks to your most noble parts. The
book starts and ends with the premise that you are first and foremost a child of God, and as such, your true happiness emerges
from your ongoing relationship with God.

Retirement, then, is yet another forum where you can perform a
new act in the drama of your life, becoming ever more the person
that God intends you to be. You are the writer, the director, and the
actor or actress in this new production. Study these pages well;
they offer you a script for genuine peace and purpose.

Retirement: The Great Experiment

Two separate trends are converging to create the greatest demographic experiment we have ever seen. First, people are retiring earlier than they ever have before. The average retirement age has declined from around sixty-five, some fifteen years ago, to around fifty-eight today. Second, people are living longer; the longevity of our total population, in fact, continues to rise. Males today can expect to live an average of seventy-two and a half years, while females can expect to live almost five years beyond that. Every indication is that these numbers will continue to rise.

This new wave is silently sweeping our society and our Church. We are aging! No, not just individually, but culturally—in our society, in our population. This process can be seen in two ways. First, the number of maturing persons is growing faster than any other segment of our population. Second, the percentage of our population that is over sixty-five years of age is also growing. We are getting older, absolutely and relatively.

This is not a tragedy for our culture. On the contrary, it's a bonanza, if we can truly squeeze from our retirement years all the potential for personal and individual achievement that is there. If the "armies" of retirees can be inspired to address some of the cultural problems that plague our society today—if we can find the motivation to begin addressing these problems—there is no doubt that radical changes can be accomplished, changes that we have never been able to successfully tackle before.

Today's retirees are unlike any other group that has come along so far. Retirees are healthier by far, wealthier, better educated, and more skilled. Today's retirees have vitality, verve, desire, personal direction, and deeper insight than our society has heretofore experienced. The group, if they can be seen as a group, is a power-packed potential of achievement, practical problem solving, enlightened wisdom, and focused energy. Here is one of the most pressing challenges of our time; here is where our pioneering spirit of exploring new territory can manifest itself in ways never before possible. The challenge is how to harness the phenomenal resources resident in this talented, resourceful, seasoned, and faith-filled population we call retirees.

Age is not a criterion for a successful retirement. Age alone offers no guarantee that we'll gather the necessary wisdom to exploit the opportunities of retirement and find the happiness waiting there as undiscovered treasure. Age does not miraculously give us the requisite tools, competencies, knowledge, and attitudinal shifts to ensure that our retirement will proceed maximally. Some people have thirty years of experience, and others have one year of experience thirty times.

Retirement does not necessarily mean cessation from all work. I've had people come up to me and say, "Well, I'm not retired-retired." This means that they are probably retired from their long-held primary means of making a living, but they are still working at "bridge job" or even retirement job.

The Department of Labor offers two criteria that must be fulfilled before an individual can be considered "retired." First, a person must be working less than full time to be considered retired, and the Department of Labor considers full time to be forty hours or more. The second criterion is that the person must be receiving *some portion* of their regular income from a pension or pensionlike vehicle. This can be a private savings IRA-type plan, a company pension, an annuity, or social security payments. This means that a person could work up to 39+ hours a week, receive as little as 5 percent of his or her total income from a pension, and be considered retired for legal purposes. The point is that persons can still be working, even substantially, and still be considered retired.

The journey from full-time work to full-time retirement in its traditional sense may take years to accomplish; there is no rush! The question for preretirees, especially those who are people of faith, is: "To what degree during this time am I actively and consciously encountering the personal growth tasks and individual challenges that I need to address if I am to achieve the maturity necessary to really get the most out of retirement?"

Retirement means many different things to many different people. Some retirees embrace their new lifestyle generously. They seem to revel in their newfound freedom, thrive in their new activities and new relationships, and celebrate in their good fortune to be alive in this marvelous time of life. Other retirees appear indifferent about retirement. While not forlorn, they seem somewhat lusterless, slightly distressed, and occasionally irritable beyond what could be considered normal. Still other retirees seem repelled by the uncertainties or the monotony of a life that seems to them empty of challenge, action, and excitement. Something has drained from them; they appear to simply survive, not genuinely thrive, in their new life.

Some of the people you may think are the most prepared to "take the plunge" into retirement turn out to be the very ones who find a retirement lifestyle to be the roughest. At some level they use denial, avoidance, anger, irritability, depression, submission, and other techniques to resist the changes that retirement brings.

This brings us to a somewhat perplexing question: What is retirement supposed to be? Is it a rest? a new career? a playground? a withdrawal? a new stimulation? a respite? Actually, there is a great deal of ambiguity surrounding retirement; we really don't know exactly what retirement is supposed to be. There are few if any social directives in our culture that guide us in organizing our retirement with stability.

There is great hope inherent in retirement, however: hope for new life prospects, new life directions, new endeavors. Retirement is a commencement. Remember when you graduated from high school, you went through commencement exercises. In my younger years I truly thought that commencement meant that something was over. Years later I realized that the event I thought was the end was actually the hopeful beginning of something different. In a very real sense, retirement is like high-school graduation: certainly an end, but also a beginning of something much bigger than you can conceive.

The Spiritual Thread

A spiritual thread runs through all the needs of retirees, a thread of pursuing peace and finding purpose. It is this thread of the Spirit that has the power to transform an ordinary retirement into an exceptional journey of discovery and intrigue, a lackluster retirement experience into a thriving adventure, a floundering retiree into a focused participant in the ongoing ministry of Jesus Christ, and a dispirited individual into an inspired reservoir of health and wellness.

Retirement holds up a new prospect of growth for us. Retirement is a new journey, a path full of challenges, where we are called to become more interesting, more curious, more personal, more diverse, and more meaningful in all that we do. As we walk this new path we need light, like headlights, to pierce into the darkness of the unknown and give us confidence. This light is the same one that has been with us all along; it is the light of Christ. Along this path we will find our true selves. We will find the dream that lies deep within, the dream that, when brought to the surface, will allow us to find a fulfillment and happiness we have seldom known before. Christ is with us in the retirement years the same way he has been with us throughout our earthly journey; the difference is that we, in our advancing wisdom, can discern his movement within more clearly, more surely.

For the Church, retirees represent a ministerial potential of unlimited proportion. Today's retirees are the folks who laid the cornerstones of our churches, brought their children for baptism, built schools, and enrolled their children and saw them confirmed and married. Today these same people are heralding their grandchildren, and even great-grandchildren, to meet Jesus, and to help new generations come to know themselves as children of God.

These are people of faith—and their numbers are rising. It's not uncommon to see churches with congregations in which 30 and even 40 percent of the people are retired. Here lies the power of the Church. Their hearts hold the passion of the Spirit, the enthusiasm of the apostles, the vitality of our saints, and the determination of our martyrs.

Yet retirees have their own human and spiritual developmental needs. They cannot be expected to spiritually feed themselves. They need the nurturance of the Church in their lives as much as they always have, but in different ways. These rising needs present themselves as opportunities for our parishes and churches. Our Church needs to reach out to its retirees in new ways that can serve as cohesive forces in their individual and collective lives.

Retirement challenges us in ways we have not yet experienced. Retirement offers invitations for spiritual and personal growth that can transform us, drawing us closer to God and to our true selves. The power that drives this transformation process is the power of love.

These challenges of retirement are most keenly seen on a spiritual level. They involve the distinction between the forces of light, that we call love, and the forces of darkness, that we call fear. Love inspires us to shape our beliefs in the direction of peace. Love affords us a keener awareness of the truth within ourselves and in our world. Love invigorates our thinking so we can find fuller respect to the point of reverencing all that God has made. We wake up! Fear, on the other hand, lulls us to sleepwalk through life.

Fear is the opposite of love; fear pushes us toward self-absorption and causes us to criticize, find fault, and rashly judge ourselves and others. Love, on the other hand, offers us closer relationships—more intimacy in the form of true human sharing. Fear drives us to be demanding in our relationships, whereas love centers our decisions—the choices of our free will—on the spiritual realm of our beings. Whereas fear makes our decisions egocentric and self-serving, love allows us to embrace compassion and empathy. Fear allows us only to react to life; life acts on us! But love allows us to respond to life in a proactive way; we go out and greet it, welcome it.

Finding peace and purpose in our retirement means that we seek the light of love in our daily lives. If we wish the full measure of our own giftedness to blossom in our retirement, we need to heed the call of our faith and meet these challenges on the deepest level available: the spiritual level.

God is purposeful. God allows retirement to exist. Therefore, retirement must have a purpose. In retirement, as in all of life, we are called to expand our capacity for living and loving fully. Each day of our lives we are called to learn how to love better than we did yesterday. Retirement, then, is our new curriculum for learning how to love in ways that have never occurred to us, nor have ever opened up to us before. The central question for the Christian retiree is: "How can I learn to love better today?" The answer to this question propels us on a daily enterprise of cosmic proportions, a thrilling adventure of delight, awe, and peace. Here is the gift and the challenge that retirement offers to us.

In the many retirement workshops I've given over the past ten years, I have undoubtedly learned more from the participants than they possibly could have learned from me. I'd like to end this introduction with three definitions of retirement written through a group process at one of these workshops. I am proud of these definitions, because each one captures different facets of the essence of "retirement as a spiritual journey."

1. Retirement is that purifying gift and stage of adult life inviting us to summarize and integrate the meaning of who we've become, as a reflection of God's love.

2. Retirement is the point in life when we see the events, circumstances, and relationships that have filled the chalice of life from a higher vantage point. Retirement is designed to be a time of offering to God our total selves. Retirement is the phase when hopes and dreams can be actualized, free from the structures that would hinder personal and spiritual growth.

3. Retirement is a time when we change our focus from "doing" to "being," a time for shedding some of the unnecessary trappings for a more simple existence, while remaining involved in the mission of the Church—be that in prayer, in presence, or in patient-hood.

P.S. To learn how to bring a retirement ministry to your church or organization, and to learn how you can become a trained "retirement consultant," see page 133.

RICHARD P. JOHNSON, PH.D.

CHAPTER 1

Let Go!

To let-go is not to deny, but to see reality more accurately...
to fear less, and love more.

ANONYMOUS

Retirement Success Pearl #1

Career Reorientation: The degree to which you are able to psychologically let go of your full-time job as your primary source of self-identity, and can emotionally take on other activities (recreational, social, spiritual) that support your self-esteem in terms of a new life definition.

Retirement Challenge #1: How do I redefine myself in a unique way when I am no longer actively engaged in my former work?

Phil's Tragedy: Work As Top Priority

From the window of his fifth-floor hospital room, Phil stared out at the busy five-lane thruway off in the distance. Perplexing questions emerged through his muddled thoughts: "What happened? Why am I here in the psychiatric section? How could I be suffering from depression, when I had never felt this way ever before? How can I get myself out of this mess?"

Phil had been an extremely loyal employee. For thirty-one years he worked for a large international corporation where he had quickly moved himself up from a mailroom clerk to a supervisor of considerable status and power. He and his wife, Margaret, had a good marriage; they raised four children and were proud of them.

Phil remembered the day, so many years ago, when his partner at work first referred to him as a "workaholic." He didn't know what it meant that day, but over time he came to understand that, in truth, his primary focus in life was his work. Margaret and the kids had long ago realized that Dad's work took first place in his life. Phil loved his wife and children, it's just that work was so compelling; it became his highest priority. Even when he wasn't at work, Phil still thought about "work." Weekends and vacations were sometimes hard on Phil, because he didn't have his "work" to organize his life and fill his mind.

Then, after thirty-one years, Phil was offered an "early retirement" financial incentive package. At first Phil balked, but then, with calculator in hand, he accepted the money and convinced himself that he deserved the rest that retirement could bring. Now, six months later, Phil was under the care of a psychiatrist for depression.

In his new life phase of retirement, Phil couldn't shift his thinking about himself. Throughout his entire life he had seen himself as a worker, a breadwinner, and doer of deeds—a dynamo of accomplishment. These beliefs shaped everything he perceived about himself: all his thinking, his feelings, his decisions, and ultimately his every action. Phil saw himself as a work machine. When retirement finally did come, he was unable to reclarify his perception, redesign his thinking, reshape his feelings, recast his decisions, and recommit his actions. He was unable to let go of what was, and find the "new" in him.

The Call of Retirement

As Christians, we are called to lifelong conversion, to redemption, and to transformation. We are called to reframe ourselves each day. As enlightened humans, and as committed Christians, we cannot stand still; we either grow or we stagnate; we either continue to challenge ourselves or we begin to regress into ill health of some kind.

Retirement calls us to reframe ourselves, to redefine ourselves in ways identifiably different from any shifts in our self-definition that have ever come before. Phil simply couldn't redefine himself; he couldn't disengage.

Some retirees reframe themselves by disengaging not only from their full-time work lives, but from all of life. In such a scenario, personal reframing does indeed take place, but it's hardly the healthy, growthful reframing that is positive, constructive, and enriching. On the contrary, it seems regressive, submissive, and decidedly nongrowthful. Such a retiree becomes the so-called "couch potato." For such persons, retirement is a time for slowing down—so much so that they actually come to a stop. Their energy, vitality, and direction erodes, and they become sluggish, unresponsive, inert.

Other retirees seek to continue in life just the way they did before. They simply switch activities: a sales career for the golf course; a professional engineering career for boating; a teaching career for travel; a carpenter's career for gardening. What often doesn't change is the work ethic value system that drives the activity. Sales persons take their competitive values out on the golf course; engineers take their perfectionistic values out on the boat; and so on. There is no redefinition, no reframing of self; these people simply switch one activity for another. Instead of playing one round of golf, as they did before retirement, they now play two, just to prove to themselves (and others) that they're still "OK." Where's the personal growth?

As Christian retirees who want to find robust fulfillment in retirement, we need not take either route: the disengagement route or the continuity of activities route. Rather, we can take the personal growth and development route. We do, of course, want to follow our instincts and remain strenuously engaged in the mainstream of life. Naturally, it may not be possible to remain as physically engaged in life as we would like, or to the degree that we formerly enjoyed. Maturity can erode our physical strength, stamina, and sensitivity of yesterday. Yet it *is* always possible to make choices that keep us in the mainstream of life regardless of our physical condition. Reframing ourselves in our retirement years may eventually mean that we need to find a new life mainstream.

Disengagement

Early in our lives we develop an image of ourselves, an image that we grow into. Throughout our life span, this image is constantly undergoing modification. Some of us find modification easier than others. Some of us stand rigidly on a narrowly defined image of ourselves and give permission for only minor changes to this original image. These are the people who find the life transition into retirement somewhat difficult. Putting a new frame around ourselves can be threatening.

Personal reframing necessarily involves some form of disengagement. It's these disengagements in life that we find the most challenging. One wise person once commented that personal change is so difficult, not because opening new doors is hard, but because it's so hard to close the "old" doors—and retirement necessarily means that we close doors. Our work life, that so heavily defined what we were in our full-time working years, is gone; the door is closed. This change requires that we mourn the personal loss, but it also demands that we construct a new image of ourselves, a new definition of self.

Retirement usually means that we are no longer a full-time worker, a full-time professional. We can no longer define ourselves in relation to our employer. We no longer have the status that came with the occupational position we once filled. All of these closing doors push us to open new ones, doors that give us new definitions of self, new descriptions of what we are. We have an innate need to see ourselves as something; it is this image that defines what we are, if not who we are. It is precisely this image of ourselves that must be *re*constructed in *re*tirement.

Who Are We...Really?

As we strip away our former self-definition, we grow closer and closer to discovering who we really are. This is the first challenge of retirement. We come to see ourselves more clearly. As we venture deeper into this challenge of retirement, we come to realize that the uniqueness about ourselves that formerly came from the outside is actually emerging from within—from our spiritual nature. In our working years we derived much of our uniqueness from things like our job title, our way of doing things, our methods of tackling new projects, the special ways we approached our work. When the doors to this source of self-definition are closed in retirement, we look for other doors, passageways to new life, new dreams, new purpose.

Losses are at the core of any transition. Indeed, retirement can be seen as our personal story of how we give up some things and take on others. The first thing that retirement forces us to give up is the image of our own selves. Disengagement is a necessary part of life; disengagement is at the heart of conversion, redemption, and transformation. So many times the pain of disengagement is simply too much for some retirees. They fail to embrace the loss that is inherent in disengagement, they push it away. In so doing, they miss the opportunity of engaging in new life.

The shift in self-definition that this first retirement challenge requires is not easy. Our worldly culture constantly reminds us that we are what we *do*. Our culture is blind to the reality of our spiritual nature and concentrates almost entirely on our worldly utility. When Jesus asks Peter, "And who do you say that I am?" he is asking the same question that we as retirees ask of ourselves: "Who do you say that I am?" The answer to this question is the "stuff" of this first challenge.

Challenges Seek Resolutions

Challenges seek resolutions. Healthy resolution of this first retirement challenge means that we shift from asking ourselves "What am I?" to asking "Who am I?" We consequently move away from an external, material, achievement, definition of self, toward a more personal, genuine, intimate and certainly spiritual definition of self. As we traverse this challenge, we come to recognize our inherent worthiness as unique persons, as unique children of God, immensely lovable just the way we are. Successful resolution means we come to see ourselves, first and foremost, as spiritual entities.

Inability to redefine ourselves in retirement has two unfortunate consequences. First, we may continue to view ourselves from an external perspective, and define ourselves on a material plane alone. This definition will prove increasing deficient and shallow. A sense of "something missing" may emerge in us, faintly at first, growing to proportions that can ultimately rob us of our peace and emotional stability.

Second, and perhaps as a consequence of the first, inability to redefine ourselves, inability to disengage from our former life and take on the new one, places us at risk of lapsing into living a submissive, lackluster life where we exist unconnected to the love-power of God. Our internal direction, focus, perseverance, stamina, and the like seem to erode away, leaving us adrift on a sea of unknowing.

One place where we find a sad commentary on the fact that some retirees, especially men, have a difficult time sculpting a new self-definition entering retirement is in suicide statistics. The highest suicide rate by far can be found among Caucasian men, aged seventy-two and older. Our media have focused on teen suicide, and rightfully so, since it seems a double tragedy that a young person would end his or her life. Yet it's retired men who succeed in ending their lives voluntarily more than anyone else.

George Eastman, founder of Eastman-Kodak Company, ended his life just two months after his retirement. He left a note that ominously read: "My work is done, why wait!" Eastman suffered from cancer at the time and was evidently experiencing considerable pain. Nonetheless, this tragic endnote dramatically portrays the extreme stretch it is for some retirees to let go of their former definition of self as "worker" and shift to a new formulation.

Our culture seems to socialize males particularly to be rather singularly focused in their life. Males learn that their purpose in life is to work. Females are instructed to work as well, yet females are given a second important, self-defining role; they are "trained" to be caregivers. When retirement comes, females retain their caregiving role to support themselves psychologically.

Retirees—males and females—who are so crystallized in their former "worker" roles and can't seem to carve out another role, can find themselves feeling adrift, unfocused, and eventually purposeless. Such retirees are at risk of falling prey to one of an array of maladies, such as depression (or at least dispirited emotions, what mental health professionals sometimes call the "walking wounded"), irritability, apathy, self-absorption, interpersonal distancing, anger—the list of possibilities goes on and on. Some retirees, like Mr. Eastman, go to the extreme of taking their lives into their own hands. For such persons the retirement lifestyle becomes a prison, a confinement where their former means of self-expression is muzzled; they are left forlorn, and gradually move into despair. They consider their life to be over, finished, completed. Like Mr. Eastman, they see their only option to be the next "logical" step: they exit.

Disengagement and reorientation of self is not an option in retirement; it is mandatory, and it is serious business. As we have seen, the consequences of failing to address this challenge can bring about behavioral outcomes of the most noxious form. If this reframing process is blocked, voluntarily or otherwise, we find ourselves gradually becoming stagnant, psychologically crusted, emotionally two-dimensional, and mentally frozen. When this happens, life begins to close down. We avoid situations that may confront our crystallized perception of ourselves. We deny ourselves valuable growth opportunities. We divert new streams of information away from us, and push away the very people who can serve as partners in our ongoing process of growth and development. Perhaps worst of all, we shut out God.

The personal disengagement and self-*red*efinition that retirement offers requires power. This power comes to us from the virtue of acceptance—freely and creatively accepting on God's plan for living, and giving God our total "amen." Acceptance means being in agreement with God's will, having a sense of being in accord with God, honoring God. The opposite of acceptance is dissension.

Phil's therapy needs to address his spiritual groundedness. He needs to take a bold, frontal look at himself. Eventually, he will need to forgive himself for whatever neglect his workaholism inflicted upon his wife and children. He'll need to come before God seeking forgiveness for these transgressions and making strong resolve to redirect his life away from the narrow image he formerly had of himself. He will need to reconstruct an image of himself that reflects the genuine "godly" reality that is his true self.

Acceptance vs. Dissension

Acceptance is the power that motivates us to address this first retirement challenge. Acceptance means being in agreement with God's will, having a sense of being in accord with God, honoring God. There is no hint of resignation or submission in acceptance. Acceptance is power, true spiritual "grit." It's the opposite of dissension, becoming disagreeable and contrary. When we dissent, we fight, and whenever we fight we eventually become depleted in some way.

Affirmation

Lord, help me to see that my retirement is a commencement… a new beginning. Help me truly understand the opportunity that I have been given by my retirement. Help me transform my view of myself from one that is primarily based on my functional, wage-earner self, to a greatly expanded image of who I am; your spiritual child. Help me to reframe myself. Let my retirement become much more than switching one life activity for another; let it usher in an entirely new life for me. Dear Lord, let my life in retirement become your life. May I disengage from my old definition of self and take on a new one, a more accurate one, that fits me. Help me see who I am more clearly than I ever have before.

CHAPTER 2

Reframe Your Attitudes

Our attitudes are the mother of our actions.

R. P. JOHNSON

Retirement Success Pearl #2

Retirement Value: The degree to which you can re-frame your attitudes to give worth and significance to retirement as a meaningful time in life.

Retirement Challenge #2: What is the value of retirement? Of what use will I be in my retirement years if I'm not working?

Bill's Story: Hidden Retirement Fears

Bill sat reminiscing about his retirement party. What a joyous occasion! He had told everyone that he loved the idea of retirement. "Imagine," he said, "being paid for not working." He just couldn't wait to try out his new golf clubs and fishing rod. He relished the idea of being able to "sleep in" on a Monday morning. His exuberance at the party, however, seemed to somehow predict a sad paradox that was now unfolding in his life. He now realized that the euphoria he displayed at his retirement party was really a show designed to disguise the deeper, darker side of his well-hidden attitudes about retirement.

Bill actually harbored mixed feeling about retirement because of the unfortunate experiences he had seen in his dad when he retired many years ago. Even during the party Bill was aware of the thoughts that rocketed through his mind, remembering how dismal his father's retirement had been. Retirement seemed to change his father from a man in charge of his life into a submissive patient who required assistance for everything. Bill remembered how his opinion of his father had fallen considerably after he had retired.

Today Bill wondered whether his retirement reaction was somehow genetic. Like his father before him, Bill didn't feel the same level of confidence he had when he was working. His sense of himself seemed to have tumbled, and he was concerned, even frightened. Of course, Bill didn't tell anyone about his doubts, not even his wife, Barb. He simply let his confusing attitudes about retirement turn his own experience into a trial of forbearance, rather than an opportunity to pursue the effortless lifestyle he had so blithely imaged.

Predetermined Biases

When we arrive at retirement we bring our predetermined biases with us. Unfortunately, many of us associate retirement with personal loss, not gain; aging, not renewed youthfulness; death, not new opportunity. Such bias can dramatically cloud our retirement experience. We seem to live normal lives, and we may even appear to enjoy our new lifestyle, yet our underlying negative beliefs about retirement may be blocking a good part of the value of retirement from hitting home. We often conclude, perhaps subconsciously, that happiness in retirement is for others, but certainly not for us, because our beliefs equate happiness and personal worth with working.

Where do these beliefs and attitudes about retirement come from? Actually our perception of how others—our parents, relatives, friends, coworkers—handled their retirement contributes to our beliefs and expectations about our own retirement. Bill's model of retirement was heavily flavored by his father's experiences. No matter what Bill may have thought on a rational, logical level, lurking deep in his imprinted beliefs about retirement were unhealthy memories of how his father, now long deceased, had fallen apart.

John Powell, S.J., a noted author and talented speaker, says that an attitude is "a lens of the mind through which we perceive reality over and over again in exactly the same way." Attitudes and beliefs, then, are at the epicenter of all our human action.

To what degree do we value retirement as a human stage of development? Do we see retirement being as valuable and personally growth-filled as our twenties, thirties, forties, fifties? Does our conception of retirement somehow demean, downgrade, or diminish our value as a human being? The degree to which any of these notions rumble through our beliefs and become actions by way of our attitudes, to that same degree will we suffer a nagging discontent in retirement.

Retirement As an Age Perceptual Shift

Retirement is the first time in our culture when we are forced to stand up, as it were, and declare ourselves "older," or at least "on the more mature side" of middle age. This admission into retirement is a high price to pay. Indeed, it becomes unbearable for some of us.

Actually there is little association between age and retirement. Attitudes about retirement are not connected to age at all. It's easy to find a young person with an exceptionally positive attitude about retirement; it's equally easy to find an older individual with clearly negative attitudes about retirement. A prevalent myth seems still alive, that the older we become the more prepared we become for successful retirement living. This is a myth! My research has uncovered fifteen factors that clearly effect our preparation for retirement. Please notice that age is not one of them.

Because no one wants to be "older," no one looks forward to being ninety-six years old, we tend to stretch middle age as long and as far as we possibly can. Our culture has some very ageist ideas about our later years and, unfortunately, retired folks are not immune from these myths. Feelings of inferiority and lack of self-esteem are all too common emotional reactions to "getting older." I once was taken aback after I innocently referred to a gentleman as a "senior citizen." He indignantly rebuffed my remark saying, "I'm not a senior citizen, I'm a 'seasoned' citizen." Even the rather benign title of "senior" bothered this man; he wanted to avoid all references to his chronological status.

Such ideas are stereotypes of aging picked up from earlier times when "old" was synonymous with "bad," or at least "unfortunate." Certainly there is nothing bad or unfortunate about being "older," or being an "elder." Such notions are less than positive only in the minds of unenlightened individuals who are developmentally stuck in a previous stage of life and refuse to open their minds to another point of view. Yet our attitudes about aging persist; some of us continue to see aging as a personal injury of profound proportion—an injury too hurtful for some of us to bear.

Thankfully, not all retirees share such negative biases. However, enough retirees do harbor such thinking that their desires for a positive and exceptional retirement are sometimes neutralized or impacted negatively. God wants retirement to make a difference in the lives of all retirees of faith, yet positive ideas about retirement simply don't register for some of us. What to do? The solution to such thinking is change. Retirement requires change, sometimes tremendous change!

New Thinking About Change

We need new thinking about change, especially the change that successful retirement requires; we need a departure from the old paradigm. Instead of viewing change as an end-result, for example, we need to see change as a series of developmental steps or stages taken by individuals on an ongoing basis. Change, like success, is more a journey than a destination. Change of any sort is created by the gradual and logical consequence of innumerable modifications, shifts, turns, personal alterations, and modulations. All of this happens in the personal arena before it has an ultimate impact in the retirement lifestyle. Retirees need to learn the competencies of change well before the beginning of their retirement experience.

Retirement specialists maintain that effective change first occurs in the attitudinal level of individuals. This means that a shift in values, or at least a modification of beliefs, is required before we can effectively incorporate new visions of what is next in our life. We have to assemble these new visions in a manner that paves the way for eventual healthy change. This new thinking asserts that retirees and preretirees will function best under conditions of change when they have the tools, skills, competencies, and knowledge necessary to inject this new way of thinking into their lives.

The sometimes excruciating tumult that has greeted the American retiree in past years has, if nothing else, successfully shifted the center of responsibility for change from the shoulders of the employer to the employee—where it needs to be and, frankly, where it can do the most good. We are all in charge of our own retirement; we craft it ourselves, and our attitudes and beliefs will inspire the master architect of our retirement lifestyle.

By definition, retirees need to become change specialists. Unfortunately retirees have seldom been sufficiently equipped to handle the breadth and depth of change thrust at them. They have had few of the tools for change they needed. They have had no operating system which connected the tools together into a meaningful and functional whole. As a consequence, some significant percentage of retirees have ventured into this new developmental stage less than fully prepared for the level of changes that are bearing down on them. Some retirees erroneously think that by retiring they will escape the intense pace of change that has characterized American business. These people will be disappointed, because retirement presents an entirely new "bag of changes," unlike any they have yet encountered.

Change, the necessary change that enables retirees to become thriving as people and as children of God, has eluded the very retirees who need change the most. The vibrant and encouraging opportunities for transforming change that retirement brings with it have been missed by too many retirees, even those preretiring individuals who confidently and boldly announced their visions of "good retirement" at their retirement parties. Many retirees do not reap the benefits of their visions for change, because they did not know how to follow through by practicing the competencies of change.

Personal Growth: The Ultimate Value of Retirement

Just as maturation (aging) *requires* change, it *offers* growth. The growth that personal maturation offers is an internal growth, a growth in spirit, in love, in the intangibles of living. Growth in our later years requires a shift in perception and a growth in our personal compassion and sensitivity that is identifiably different from what was required in our earlier years.

Healthy resolution of this second challenge in our spiritual journey of retirement requires that we see ourselves as developmentally engaged in a vital adventure in soul enrichment, searching for deeper and deeper aspects of our true, holy selves. This includes seeing retirement as full of options for personal growth, developing a healthy focus on our inner selves, knowing that our interior is now the new frontier for development. Healthy resolution of this challenge involves a shift away from the external world as our primary arena for growth, and a corresponding entry onto a new forum for growth—a less tangible forum, but one offering far more riches than the previous arena. Retirement offers a new understanding of what it means to "lay up treasures in heaven rather than on earth."

Unhealthy resolution of success factor #2 leads to a view of ourselves as useless, that retirement has no value at all, that we are "washed-up" and have no purpose. This is precisely what Bill was beginning to realize about his own malaise. Such a regressive perspective serves only to bring on the number one emotional malady of retirement: depression.

If we let it, retirement can cleave us from ourselves as well as from our career. Our work gave us power, status, and a sense of purpose in life. Unless we can meet this second challenge with a healthy resolution, we risk falling prey to a loss more devastating than loss of work; we can lose our very selves. Our retirement transition will then become much more than a role exchange; it will demand that we forfeit our very selves.

Vision vs. Blindedness

Vision is the power that serves to bolster healthy growth in this second challenge. Vision enables us to look past the physical plane to view the glory of God's plan and purpose for our life right now. Vision allows us to see the beauty and goodness that is there for those who wish to glimpse it. Vision means discerning the glory of heaven right here on earth; seeing the world as a place where God's will eventually prevails. Vision bestows love in abundance.

Blindedness is the opposite of vision. Blindedness means that we figuratively grope in the dark, we cannot see where we are going. When we are blinded, we find ourselves visionless and hoodwinked by erroneous attitudes, that are unfounded in reality. Blindedness impairs our vision, limiting our vision and diminishing our horizons.

Affirmation

Lord, help me to rise above the world's definition of retirement and embrace a new vision of retirement. Help me see retirement as abundance, as wonder, and as new hope. I want to shift my attitude about retirement from one of loss to one of gain. Help me value retirement as part of your plan for me, dear Lord.

CHAPTER 3

Take Charge

You are creating it all. Nobody else is doing it to you.
WAYNE DYER, PH.D.

Retirement Success Pearl #3

Personal Empowerment: The degree to which you can take charge of your life and rely on your own internal sense of self-discernment for making plans and decisions.

Retirement Challenge #3: How will I organize the structure of my life without work?

The Need to Take Charge: Doctor Joe

Joe was a physician's physician. It seemed that he had always wanted to be a doctor, for as long as he could remember. Certainly by high school his career focus was clear. Every step he took, every class, every part-time job, every extracurricular event— even his choices for athletics: all were undergirded by his goal of one day becoming a doctor. Such a clear vision of the future actually made Joe's life rather predictable; most of his decisions were already made for him. He simply needed to jump through the right hoops, as it were.

When Joe finally did receive his M.D., his next career steps were settled. He joined a growing practice that had pursued him and, in a short time, Joe had a full patient load. He was living his dream; all his hard work had paid off. He was a doctor; he was respected and had status in the community. He could look forward to a lifetime of security in medicine.

Joe arranged his entire life around medicine. His family life, social life, relationships, self-esteem, and leisure were all dictated by his allegiance to and reverence for medicine. Once again, Joe had few personal decisions to make; his profession made them for him. His life, it seemed, was on autopilot, with the demands of medicine sitting in the cockpit directing every aspect of life.

Yet Joe never complained. After all, he was exactly where he wanted to be. He actually enjoyed all the "perks" of being a doctor.

During his middle years, however, Joe would occasionally feel an unwelcome sensation in the form of a question, like "Is something missing?" He couldn't think of anything that he didn't have, though; everything was in place—just like it always had been.

Years passed and middle-aged Joe evolved into later middle age, right into preretirement. It was becoming rather uncomfortably common now for Joe to encounter fellow doctors who would "throw out" that terrible, almost insulting question: "So Joe, isn't it about time for retirement?" Although Joe would reel back from the question, he took the thought seriously, because he could see the writing on the wall; his days of being a full-time active physician were numbered. Certainly Joe was financially prepared; he had been contributing to retirement-investment plans for years.

Eventually, running out of excuses for not retiring, Joe was all but pushed into retirement, because it simply seemed the "thing to do." On that first Monday morning of his retirement, though, Joe awoke with an acute feeling of emptiness. He didn't know what to do. He felt lost, with no sense of direction, no call to action, no sense of himself.

For three months Joe struggled like this. Every morning seemed like just another empty vessel, giving him nothing to drink, offering no sustenance for existence. One day Joe heard of a job opening for a physician who would do nothing but give physicals, and he snapped at the opportunity without thinking twice. His days seemed less fulfilling to him, but at least he didn't have to face the awful emptiness that had haunted those horrible three months when he was "retired." Joe says he'll never retire, that there's no sense in it. Work is what he knows and work is where he'll stay.

We can call Joe a workaholic. We can call him noble for having such a highly developed work ethic. We can be amazed by his stamina, or inspired by his dedication and zeal. But I feel sorry for Joe—not sorry that he is still working, that's neither right nor wrong, personally healthy or unhealthy. I feel sorry for Joe because he's not in control of his life. Long ago Joe abdicated his decision-making power. He gave away his free will to his one mistress—and her name is medicine.

Joe forfeited his self-direction. He let situations and circumstances outside himself dictate his life. All else was secondary to the controlling force of medicine. Some would say that Joe's life is a life well invested—and it certainly is for Joe's patients. He appears selfless, endlessly giving, and dedicated. Yet, what is the mix of his motivation between love of medicine and fear of making genuine life decisions? Does Joe simply distrust the direction he could give his life, allowing an outside force, in his case medicine, make all his life decisions for him?

Our Need to Order Life

How might we be like Joe? Even though Joe appears very much "in charge," he isn't. We all have needs for order and organization in our lives. The question is: "Are we the designer of this order and organization, or do we actually shunt this lifelong function of self-direction onto other persons, other outside forces?" The degree to which we allow some outside force to drive our life is the degree to which we are not living our own life, but someone else's. If Joe's primary motivation and guiding principle for practicing medicine was a real dedicated, compassionate, and even spiritual quest for serving humankind altruistically, then that would be quite different from what was actually the case for Joe. He simply had not given himself any practice in directing his own life. Joe was blindly following the dictates of a profession, following a rather predictable and preengineered course. The only decision Joe made was stepping onto the "moving sidewalk" career track of the medical profession. Every decision after that was predetermined. He needed to invest no personal volition in the process after that point; one decision had been made, and one decision was all it took!

All of us need to fashion our own lives in unique ways. Each of us has been gifted by God, and these gifts demand expression, otherwise we find ourselves becoming more and more unhappy. Many of us grow accustomed to finding a forum for expressing our gifts in our work life. When retirement takes away this forum, however, we may be left feeling rather naked—unless we have developed the capacity of taking charge of our lives in a more complete way.

We quite naturally inject into our lives a certain style of action, a way of operating in the world that is ours alone. This "style" gives us our sense of self, a distinctiveness that is all ours. This search for distinctiveness is a reflection of the uniqueness that God has gifted to each of us without measure. How wonderful is this mystery! Our very divinity is real and seeks expression individually. We are charged by our birth, our very existence, to pursue this authenticity of self throughout our lives. We must never stop discovering and developing this wonderful uniqueness God has given us.

This specialness that is ours alone requires many forums; it cannot be confined to our work arena, because we are much too diverse in our gifts. Joe, as well intentioned as he was, had confined his uniqueness, his individual style, to medicine. Beyond medicine, Joe's gifts lay fallow, because he couldn't find the self-direction, the self-empowerment, to make things happen anyplace else. Joe was developmentally lopsided. His contorted handicap kept him from taking charge of his full life. While his career arena was overdeveloped, his other five arenas remained wanting: family, relationships, self, spiritual, and leisure.

When Joe so haplessly stumbled into retirement, he immediately felt unsteady, unsure, inferior, and lacking in any form of self-direction. This is a sting for many retirees, but for Joe this loss felt like the jolt of an earthquake taking away the very ground beneath him. He had constructed no other platforms onto which he could safely jump when work was pulled from under him. He was out of control, and a collision within himself was inevitable.

For most of us the loss of self-direction is but subtly felt at first, when we move beyond our full-time paid work; some of us don't feel it at all. Yet losing the unique authority we exercised over the manner in which we performed our work does impact us at some level. Unless we were all but detached from our work, we found a connection with it that gave us a sense of freedom to express our unique gifts. It's not that retirement takes away our *ability* to make decisions; rather, we find ourselves without the *opportunity* to make decisions. The forum has been dismantled. Yet the need to express ourselves, to make decisions, to manifest our style or God-given gifts, remains. Here is where we rely upon our ability to take charge, to empower ourselves.

I remember a time in my life when I felt a high degree of personal empowerment. I had just completed a lengthy process of self and soul discernment, and decided to give up a rather "cushy" job to go to graduate school. My wife and I packed our two small children and all our earthly possessions into our Volkswagen and headed for the university, halfway across the country. I can still remember the mixed feelings of excitement, trepidation, and personal satisfaction I experienced those first few months of graduate school. I remember pedaling my bike home from the university and breaking into the broadest, most fulfilling smile with the thought, "I'm really here. I really did it!" Although scary, the sense of satisfying self-direction spread out from within me like a luminous glow of sheer delight. Personal empowerment, making decisions from the heart, ignites us, stimulates us, and enables us to reach deeply into our authentic selves. I often wonder how my life might have unfolded had this burst of self-empowerment not directed me toward new life goals.

Even though we call it self-direction, or personal empowerment, the process of discernment for a person of faith is not one undertaken alone. God has to be part of the process. When we go deep into ourselves to dredge the depths in search of truth, we can only go confidently with God as our partner. Without God's grace, we cannot find that changeless truth that lays dormant within.

Each decision, when made in conscious concert with God, brings us that much closer to our authentic self. I've no doubt that "my" decision to enter graduate school, thus taking the more risky path, has resulted in innumerable blessings. Chief among these blessings is the marvelous feeling of communion with God's purposes, a holy alignment between us that allows maximal growth, generativity, freedom, and happiness. This is not to say that such miraculous insight emerged immediately; it has taken many years, since that decision to enter graduate school until this very day, to realize the grand "rightness" of following the risky path. There have been more than several intervening years when personal turmoil, doubt, and longing for what had been tormented me. Yet God's grace held me steadfast. My weakness provided the entrée for God's grace and power.

The process of soul searching and alignment with God's nudgings within is a never ending one. There are few times when we can dig out such personal and spiritual gems as when we are moving toward retirement and proceed well into it. These are times when we are somewhat freer from the busyness and the responsibilities of our "doing" life and can find the courage to address the risks without undue fear of upsetting the plans and development of our children, our spouse, and our career. Here we can dig deeply into ourselves and, with our new "finds," can take the more risky path.

God wants us to know freedom—especially the ultimate freedom of finding communion with God's loving care for us. God's plan for our life unfolds ever more clearly and confidently as we keep in touch with the unique gifts God has given us. What the world might deem the straight and prudent path is generally not the path God would have us follow. It is here, in the discernment freedom of retirement, where we can more directly approach ourselves.

Without this discernment process, coupled with the freeing power of personal empowerment, we may erect a retirement marked by dissatisfaction—perhaps not a "wrong" retirement, but simply one that lacks a sense of richness and depth. Without

personal discernment and its consequent empowerment, we may
founder in a directionless sea, and there be buffeted by whatever
shifts, shoals, showers, and storms that the open sea dispenses.
We find no safe harbor without personal direction; our ship lacks
a keel that can steady us and make our way straight. We seem
to simply drift without form or function, roaming aimlessly
without cause or mission. We may find many diversions, but
without adequate discernment, each of these diversions gives
us only temporary relief from the sense of emptiness within,
that throbbing ache that is so very hard to describe and that is
sometimes hardly noticeable, while at other times is unmistak-
ably punishing.

Finding ourselves lacking an arena in which to perform, we
have no way of injecting our unique style into our lives. Our
sense of order and organization remains disturbed. We lack a
field upon which we can play; we have no track upon which to
run. Anemic self-direction skills sentence us to a life equally
lacking in wellness, wisdom, and wholeness.

When we do take the risk of discernment, through prayer,
spiritual reading, spiritual direction, retreats, sacraments, and a
true sense of longing for God's grace in our life, we enter onto
the holy path of finding God within us. We stir our spiritual pot,
as it were. We begin to see our life as a continuous prayer, an
adventure in personal enrichment and soul learning. Personal
empowerment allows us to see with new eyes and to discover
that God exists everywhere and in everyone. Here we come to
quite naturally find a path upon which we *can* dedicate our lives
to God's ongoing mission, and where genuine living resides as
well. We develop the indescribable pleasure of walking with
Jesus. In short, we discover a new kind of personal power that
we can call spiritual empowerment.

What we begin to recognize in us is a command of our personality as we never had before. We open ourselves to the grace, the
light, and the energy of God, all of which flows into our center

where our personality functions best. We discover, regardless of our physical condition, a new life, a new lightness, a rightness as we eventually approach a oneness with God. Everyday we have the choice of spiritual empowerment or personal submission. This choice is made by and through our self direction. Who and what is in charge of your life?

Strength vs. Weakness

The personal attribute that can propel our personal self-determination is the power of strength. Personal strength is the capacity for sustained, purposeful action. It is knowing that what is true can never hurt us—the attitude of being straightforward and upright. The opposite of strength is weakness.

Weakness renders us powerless, unable, and incapable. Weakness cripples us, it takes away our personal rudder making us directionless on a sea of unknowing. Weakness leaves us exhausted, shattered, and at risk for becoming demoralized.

Affirmation

Lord, help me to awaken more fully to the fact that my decisions open connections between my will and Thy Will. My discernment either separates me or bonds me to You. Help me see my gifts, and be able to express them in all that I do. Help me fully grasp my own distinctiveness, and walk confidently in your holy mystery. You made me specially, dear Lord, and granted me a uniqueness that can reflect God's love like no one else. Let me recognize the full measure of the power that You have invested in me, and let me always remain open to Your lead in discovering ways and means of using this power in Your love. I know that with my cooperation, Your sacred plan for my life will gradually unfold as it should and I will find wondrous happiness and good cheer.

CHAPTER 4

Grow Well

There's a big difference between "being sick" and "being ill."

R. P. JOHNSON

Retirement Success Pearl #4

Physical Wellness: The degree to which you can grow well and clearly perceive that you are experiencing wellness on the physical and emotional levels, and wholeness on the spiritual level.

Retirement Challenge #4: How can I thrive, not merely survive, in retirement?

The Need to Grow Well: Ethan's Epiphany

Ethan reached for his morning coffee as he gazed out the kitchen window onto the patio of the house next door. He recalled the day that his neighbor Ramon finally finished his beloved patio and threw a neighborhood barbecue to celebrate. That was before Ethan's heart attack and his consequent early retirement. Ten years has passed since then. Today Ethan finds himself mentally, if not physically, in better shape than ever before.

In his early years Ethan was a milkman, but as the dairy shrank smaller and smaller, Ethan could see the writing on the wall and applied for a job with the local utility company. He worked there for twenty years before he had to leave for health reasons. Since then, he can honestly say that what his life may lack in physical vigor, it has more than compensated for in a stimulating and rich mental, emotional, and spiritual life. Ethan knows his physical limitations. He knows he has a chronic disease, but he also knows how to take good care of it. In that sense, he feels well, even though he knows that he's sick.

Ethan looks back at those frightening days in the cardiac-care unit. They told him that he had sustained significant damage to his heart; his heart was operating at only 15 to 20 percent of its normal capacity. His life hung in the balance. As he slowly regained strength, he attributed his good fortune to competent doctors, exceptional nurses, miraculous medication, and prompt surgery. Yet, beyond all this, Ethan sees his prayers, his faith, and his walk with Jesus to be the real power behind his recovery. Even though he knows he'll never be "cured" of heart disease, he believes that he is clearly healing in his relationship with God, others, and himself.

For most of his adult life Ethan wasn't particularly healthy. Although he had moderate to good physical health, he enjoyed only minimal psychological health—and his spiritual health was almost nonexistent. Ethan simply brought the stormy contentiousness that marked his family of origin into his family life with his wife, Sarah. It seemed Ethan could only express sharp, caustic, and toxic emotions—baggage from a childhood of turmoil and contradiction. Spiritually, Ethan had pretty much closed off whatever spark of spirit was in him, because religion had been a frequent battleground for his parents.

Deep down, Ethan was a sensitive guy; Sarah knew this. She could see and feel the pain and struggle that marked Ethan's internal emotional landscape. She pined for the day when Ethan could break through the puzzling barriers that locked in the "real Ethan." Her patience and steadfastness kept the light of hope burning.

Then came the heart attack. In a strange way, it seemed to be the bulldozer that broke down Ethan's barriers, opening him up as never before. Finally, Ethan was able to reach inside to see the genuine person within. He wasn't the "bad boy" that he thought he was. He wasn't the angry man, the distant husband, the critical parent, or the passive-aggressive employee at all—not really. He realized over time that he had played these roles in his life as a defense against the deep hurt, shame, and guilt that he carried—all emotional antiques from his childhood that needed to be discarded. In a paradoxical way, Ethan felt healthier and freer than he'd ever felt before, even though he was physically impaired with heart disease. His heart attack had been his epiphany.

Health is a relative concept dependent upon our own subjective appraisal; there's a big difference between "being sick" and "being ill." Ethan, for example, was clearly dealing with a sickness: heart disease. Yet, even though he was sick, Ethan wasn't particularly ill. Illness is the emotional, psychological, and spiritual response or reaction to sickness. Ethan was responding well to his sickness; indeed it was his sickness that ushered in an entirely new level of wellness for him. In a strange way, Ethan was thankful for his heart disease—a paradox. He was sick, but his sickness was his path to wellness!

Such a perception of health requires that we see our sickness as something quite apart from who we are at our core. It requires the belief that sickness will not control the innermost core of who we are. Sickness, of course, is a loss; we lose a great deal when we're sick. Yet it's more our attitude about our sickness, and not the sickness itself, that determines our level of comfort and wellness. Chief among our assets in modifying our attitudes about health is our faith, that which gives us the healing power to transcend the limiting aspects of any sickness and create pockets of peace where there once stood granitelike monoliths of pain.

Yet health is not simply attitudinal; none of us can "will" heart disease or something like high-blood pressure to go away. Clearly, we do need to take good care of the marvelous machine of our body. With all the print space devoted to healthy lifestyles (we can hardly pick up a newspaper or magazine without reading about some research deducing new recommendations for living healthier), there are a few factors of self-health care that we need to concentrate on. Among these are the following:

1. proper nutrition
2. sufficient exercise
3. adequate sleep and relaxation
4. avoidance of tobacco
5. positive response to stress
6. maintaining ideal weight
7. moderate use of alcohol and drugs

Within each of these broad categories, of course, we can find many divergent recommendations that may, at times, seem contradictory; yet, even with these theoretical disagreements, the commonality of agreement between and among health professionals on these points of self-health care is astonishing. What matters is that we devise a self-healthcare plan and fold it into our lives in a consistent way. This means that we need to be committed to better health.

Some retirees, however, develop an attitude of "what's the use" with regard to their healthcare. They may have a chronic ailment, like arthritis or hypertension, and generally make few if any modifications in their lifestyle to accommodate the condition in a healthy way. "I've lived this long, I guess I'll continue living exactly as I am!" On the other side of the self-health care spectrum, of course, we find retirees who basically devote all their energies to caring for their bodies. Such a posture can lead to an equally imbalanced health picture. Over indulgence, if you will, in health practices can bring about a brand of self-absorption that clearly sets a person up for other health risks, and can trigger emotional upheavals, such as anxiety, depression, sadness, irritability, and anger—all of which can "fire-bomb" an otherwise successful retirement.

Balanced Health

Naturally our physical health remains important as we approach and live out our retirement years. Yet we cannot discount the tremendous impact that our emotional health has upon our bodies. For fifteen years I worked as a counselor and teacher in a family medicine residency program teaching the residents the "art" of medicine. The primary thrust of my work there was to investigate and teach the many ways that our emotional well-being, or lack of it, affects our physical health.

There is no end to how the mind interacts with the body. Wherever the patients' stress came from—work, family, relationships, or whatever—the result was the same; the tumult was expressed in their bodies. In addition to the many so-called "psychosomatic disorders," such as certain types of headaches, some back pain, gastrointestinal upsets, irritable bowel syndrome, spastic colon, insomnia, anxiety, and depression, I could clearly see the cross-over from emotional to physical health in almost every medical malady that entered my office. The impact is nothing short of astonishing.

Many studies have investigated this body-mind connection. If you'd like to learn more about this, a good place to start is with the late Norman Cousins's book titled *Head First: The Biology of Hope* (New York: Penguin Books, 1989). The content of the book is as intriguing as the title. Another book, *The Hardy Executive: Health Under Stress* (Maddi and Kobasa, Chicago: Dorsey Professional Books, 1987) outlines a fascinating research project and gives some practical issues that compute into the body-mind connection. The authors identify four characteristics that not only determine how stress will affect us but also protect us from the effects of prolonged stress: (1) commitment; (2) control; (3) challenge; and (4) connectedness. The authors concluded that those persons who can: (1) engage themselves fully; (2) feel they can influence events in their lives; (3) experience the stimulation of challenging themselves; and (4) can create and sustain good interpersonal relationships, seem to be the healthiest among us.

It's interesting to look at the opposites of these four characteristics. We could conclude that those retirees who (1) hold back and/or are alienated; (2) feel powerless; (3) feel threatened; and (4) are emotionally separated, are those who will not exhibit balanced health.

Six Conditions for Mental Wellness

Now that we've outlined the factors that influence your physical health, i.e., your body, let's jump to the next dimension of wellness: mental or psychological wellness. Psychological wellness, or wellness of mind is a mixture of many different factors ranging from genetics, to family dynamics in your childhood years, to your education, your level of insight, and your relationships. Yet if we looked at the behavioral outcomes of all these factors, we could compact psychological wellness into six items. These six are

1. Wellness includes developing a strong value system with life-giving beliefs about ourselves and our circumstances. It means developing an attitude of "I can positively affect my health."
2. Wellness means becoming aware of the beauty all around us, searching for that beauty all the time, and expecting the best. It means cultivating the life perspective that "God is everywhere and I'm going to find God."
3. Wellness means creating a foundation of positive thinking. It means becoming mindful of our patterns of thinking, and coming to a clearer understanding that "I am a child of God."
4. Wellness means clarifying and "getting in touch" with our feelings and "owning" them at the deepest levels. It means believing that "I strive for good cheer."
5. Wellness means deciding unquestionably that we have the power to choose. It means that our own will is genuinely free to take on the notion that "Every moment is mine to make decisions."
6. Wellness means that we exercise freedom of action. It means folding into our mind the fact that "I am free to act as God would have me act."

Six Conditions of Wholeness

Our final dimension of wellness is wellness of the spirit. We can call this "spiritual fitness" or, more simply, we can refer to this dimension simply as "wholeness." When we are purposefully addressing these three dimensions of wellness, we are said to be approaching "total health." Becoming whole in spirit can also be seen as having six conditions. Spiritual wholeness means reaching beyond the material plane and finding personal integrity creating the condition we call wholeness.

1. Wholeness means becoming ever mindful of God's presence in our daily routine.
2. Wholeness means becoming increasing awake to the innumerable reflections of God's love everywhere.
3. Wholeness means injecting faith and hope into our thinking.
4. Wholeness means feeling the joy and the pain of this world with the heart of Jesus.
5. Wholeness means remaining ever-open to the nudges of the Holy Spirit in our daily walk.
6. Wholeness means acting in confidence and perseverance, acceptance and forgiveness.

Obviously, wholeness is the ultimate health consciousness for Christians.

Retirement offers opportunities for approaching our own spiritual development as *the* expanding cohesive force and power in the mix of forces that make up our total health. We are continuously overlapping layers of body, mind, and spirit, and our health is the outcome of the balance we place in that mix. Our well-being depends upon an increasing awareness and deeper appreciation of the mystery of these forces.

Kindness vs. Neglect

Kindness is the power—virtue, if you want to call it by another name—that enables us to move forward with assertive confidence and become the best that we can become health-wise. Kindness means being gentle and respectful to our body, mind, and spirit, that is, giving these what they need. Kindness means learning how to expand our mind beyond the prison of the walls of this world. Kindness means giving nourishment in full measure to our entire being. The opposite of kindness is neglect.

The opposite of kindness is neglect. Neglect means to give little attention or respect, to disregard. Neglecting your wellness means that you're careless, lax, heedless, negligent, and inattentive. Neglect eventually hurts you and brings disorder to your overall wellness; neglect ultimately renders you impaired on one or more levels.

Affirmation

Lord, my wellness rests in you. Let me be kind to my body, my mind, and my spirit. Enliven my perception so that I can offer all the interwoven parts of me what they need to flourish and thrive. Help me construct a retirement lifestyle that allow me to give appropriate self-healthcare to all that is in my power to influence. Let me renew my commitment to better health care on every level so that I may experience the highest level of wellness possible in body, mind, and spirit. Let me listen deeply and come to respect that my needs are requirements for me to become all that God hopes for me. Help me learn that I must be tolerant and tender to myself and not neglect myself.

CHAPTER 5

Find Your Wealth

"We've got a form of brainwashing going on in our country."
Morrie sighed. "Do you know how they brainwash people?
They repeat something over and over.
And that's what we do in this country.
Owning things is good. More money is good. More property is good.
More commercialism is good. More is good.
We repeat it—and have it repeated to us—over and over
until nobody bothers to even think otherwise."

MORRIE SWARTZ, AS TOLD BY MITCH ALBOM

IN TUESDAYS WITH MORRIE, P. 124.

Retirement Success Pearl #5

Monetary Adequacy: The degree to which you can find your wealth and believe that you have planned sufficiently for your retirement finances so you can maintain an adequate standard of living.

Retirement Challenge #5: How do I support myself and my family while remaining true to myself and my God?

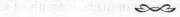

The Need to Find Your Wealth:
Mary, Harry, and the Computer

Mary looked at her checkbook. Since Harry's retirement, she had kept a separate checkbook—at his request. Actually she rather liked it, because she could keep a closer reign on her finances than when she and Harry both had access to the same account. Money was not a "problem"—not exactly. Harry had sold his business, which is what catapulted him into retirement. He received a fair sum for his life's work, and therein seemed to be one of the problems: Harry seemed obsessed with money. Each day he would spend hours hovered over his computer. When Mary would ask him what he was doing, Harry would simply respond, "I'm looking over our finances." Mary would wonder, though, what about their finances could take so much time on the computer.

The time Harry invested in the computer really wasn't a problem either. What really upset Mary was the fact that she and Harry weren't traveling, vacationing, and getting away together, as she had envisioned their retirement would involve. She felt she had postponed so much of her life with Harry, with him always "at the office." She had developed a life of her own, of course, a life that provided good friends and much satisfaction for her over the years: volunteer agencies, church organizations, civic groups, and the like. But now Mary wanted to take a turn in her life, and she was genuinely disappointed that Harry proved to be such a homebody, relentlessly glued to his finances. Slowly, Mary was resurrecting her social and volunteer life that she had hoped to move from when retirement came.

Financial Dimensions of Retirement

The financial dimensions of retirement preparation are changing. We can hardly pick up a newspaper or magazine without seeing reference to "retirement saving and investments." Actually our culture has undergone a dramatic shift in the ways we finance retirement; the burden of retirement financing is clearly shifting from the shoulders of the employer and the government, to the shoulders of the individual. This shift is having a tremendous impact on our economy and is causing us to develop greater individual savvy as investors and financial managers.

People are retiring earlier and earlier. Today the average first retirement age hovers around fifty-eight yet, the average full retirement age is about 63.5. How can this be? A clear corporate trend in the last decade has been "early out." Retirement windows, early retirement eligibility programs, and other assorted programs have the same goal: to reduce the work force. These economy-driven moves on the corporate level have caused a real reduction in the first retirement age. Yet they also have spawned another new trend; many retirees are returning to work.

Some retirees are returning to work because they need or want the money. Others are returning because they are not yet psychologically prepared for retirement; these people still need to accomplish some personal developmental tasks before they will move into full-time active retirement. It's common now to see retirees bagging groceries at your local supermarket or working behind the counter at McDonald's restaurants—and this is but the tip of the iceberg. Many retirees are finding welcoming arms at various employment sites, and not all in the service occupations. It seems that every industry is discovering the good work ethic of "senior workers" and, in many cases, are actively courting them. What goes around comes around!

A new search for personal fulfillment is another reason for the trend into so-called bridge careers, second careers, and even third careers in the years formerly thought of as belonging to retirement. I call the stage of life from age fifty-five to seventy-five the "renewal stage." The purpose of this stage is to discover new parts of ourselves that may have remained unearthed and underdeveloped. It's a time for capturing a dream that may have lived in our soul for years but was unable to come out due to the obligations that pressed in on us financially. Now, in the renewal stage, these long held-down desires can begin to flow.

For example, there's the man who started a spiritual travel company, organizing trips to ecologically unique and spiritually stimulating places. There's the woman who became a pastoral counselor at her church, finding a fulfillment she never felt in her years as an accountant. And then there's the man who became a retirement coach, helping couples find new life and new spirit. As was stated earlier, retirement does not necessarily mean stopping work. More and more "retirees" are finding themselves in positions that may have been mere undefined dreams of years earlier. They now have the time, the finances, and the experience to give their life an entirely new spin.

The basic financial question for retirement is: "How much do I need to maintain my standard of living?" Yet this question may not be easy to answer. First, we have the variable of inflation. A fixed income can vary in buying power, depending on the ongoing inflation rate. Fortunately, in recent years, this has been kept relatively in check. The other variable, of course, is how long we will live. A finite chunk of money has limits. So, "How much is enough?"

Generally, a retirement lifestyle is said to require between 70 and 80 percent of one's preretirement income. We need to replace between $700 and $800 in retirement for every $1,000 of our preretirement income. However, I know some retirees who spend 150 percent of their preretirement income, upgrading their lifestyle by travel, dining out, generous gift-giving, and more clothes-buying and leisure-time activities. Again, we see how difficult this seemingly simple question, "How much do I need?" really is.

Research on the connections between financial adequacy and well-being and life satisfaction in retirement are fairly clear.

When adequate finances are present in retirement, we see higher levels of self-esteem and personal satisfaction, otherwise known as happiness. Retirees with adequate financial means are more socially involved, participate more as volunteers, and generally register a higher sense of well-being. Financial *adequacy,* however, should not be interpreted to mean, "The more money I have the happier I will be." Such a belief is certainly not borne out in reality. Consider a man who commanded vast wealth, Howard Hughes. He found little happiness in his material wealth; indeed, he seemed in psychological and spiritual poverty.

Making decisions about retirement preparation with a calculator alone is not the best way to create a successful retirement. We are called to be good stewards, not only of our material possessions, but of our time and talents as well. Where does our true wealth lie? The world can hoodwink us into believing that retirement preparation is simply a matter of good financial planning. I hope that, after reading the rest of this book, you will find this notion to be naive and even misleading; perhaps you already do. We need to create a balance. Certainly we need to be good stewards in our financial affairs, yet we need to be vigilant and thorough in the stewardship of our mental and spiritual gifts as well. We know that human beings do not live by bread alone, but we also know that human beings certainly do need bread.

Self-Discipline vs. Self-Indulgence

The capability that drives our stewardship is self-discipline. Self-discipline means imposing order upon ourselves. It means molding our character to achieve predetermined results and placing growth and development as primary goals. The opposite or shadow of self-discipline is self-indulgence.

The opposite of self-discipline is self-indulgence. Self-indulgence is exercising little, if any personal restraint, placing no demands upon oneself. Self-indulgence is using no self-control, having no structure on one's daily lifestyle; it's becoming overly focused on consuming, seeking only "fun" experiences. Self-indulgence means one is living an imbalanced life.

Affirmation

Lord, help me to be a good steward. In retirement, help me to manage my time and my talents, as well as I manage my treasure. Help me to balance the focus I give to all of what You have given me. Never let me slip into miserliness, where I obsess on accumulating of money. Help me, dear Lord, walk the center road of self-discipline and avoiding both self-indulgence and self-repression. Your grace surrounds me with abundance; help me to access your grace and use it to stimulate the talents you have given me, in service to Your goals, Your designs, and Your direction.

CHAPTER 6

Seek Peace

*How do we experience the gladness, the delight, and the joy of life?
How do we bring about these feelings in our lives?
Whenever we personally experience joy and pleasure in life
we become aware of ourselves as enhanced and enriched.
A sense of vitality, vigor, and well-being
pervades our self-awareness.*

Sr. Mary Michael O'Shaughnessy, OP

Retirement Success Pearl #6

Present Quality of Life: The degree to which you can seek peace and find life satisfaction: personal contentment, physical health, home-life harmony, self-esteem, and spiritual integration in your life right now.

Retirement Challenge #6: How can I remain happy going into and growing through my retirement lifestyle?

The Need to Seek Peace: Chuck and Joyce

As Chuck turned into the driveway of his church, he realized that he was coming here more often these days. Trinity had been his church for many years, certainly well before his retirement five years ago.

Chuck retired from a multinational corporation, where he had worked himself up to an administrative level; he'd been there twenty-seven years. Chuck had enjoyed his work; he was well respected and received many accolades for his accomplishments. But today, as he got out of his car and headed for the pastor's office, he could honestly say that he never felt better about himself and his life in general. He had his health; he felt financially secure; his children were grown and generally doing well—some better than others.

Beyond all his good fortune, however, Chuck would say that two things matter most to him at this stage in life: his relationship with his wife, Joyce, and his relationship with God. Actually, in Chuck's mind, these two features of his current life are so overlapped as to be almost one. He knows this isn't "intellectually understandable," yet his love for Joyce has matured and emerged in his life almost as a spiritual thing. The overlap surprises even him.

Chuck wanted to talk with the pastor about some ideas he has for Trinity's senior adult ministry club called "Daytimers." Chuck and Joyce had organized the group, and it was proving to be a success. The group took trips, went to movies, had a book discussion group, and even took vacations together. The members had jelled well and Chuck and Joyce took much joy from their interactions in it. Chuck's agenda with the pastor included ways of accenting the spiritual dimensions of the group. Chuck had worked up a proposal and was confident that the pastor would "sign off" on it. As he strode down the hall toward the pastor's office, Chuck realized that developing proposals and presenting them to committees for approval was a skill he had used many times in his day-to-day work responsibilities. It felt good to Chuck to be doing it again; it gave him a sense of worthiness and utility.

Yet this feeling of utility was not the reason Chuck enjoyed his senior adult ministry. Rather, Chuck enjoyed interacting with members of the group. Certainly, he had interacted with people during his active working years, but interaction among the Day-timers was of a different caliber; it was deeper, more personal, more fulfilling. Chuck enjoyed sharing his life and his faith walk with others in the group—and he enjoyed hearing about their's as well. There was something close and warm, tender and caring, peaceful and compassionate, about the interaction in the group. He could see the changes in himself and in the other members as they became more trusting in the psychological safety that had emerged among them, especially in the past year. Chuck also realized that he and Joyce had become closer, more mutual, and more respectful of each other. Chuck is discovering new facets of himself that he never knew existed, aspects that can provide him with a measure of happiness he has never experienced before.

Happiness...Life Satisfaction

What allows us to feel happy? What gives us satisfaction or a sense of well-being in our lives? We can divide a life into six compartments, or "life arenas." Everything we do in life falls into one or more of these six life arenas.

Life satisfaction is a global concept that refers to our internal estimate of overall contentment, peace, enjoyment. It is the use-fulness of our life right now. It is our interior appraisal of how successfully we are addressing the growth and development tasks of life. It is our ability in demonstrating optimal living patterns resulting a general state of wellness. In its most basic form, life satisfaction speaks to that personally ubiquitous question, "How am I doing in my life?"

Components of life satisfaction include: zest for living, taking responsibility for our actions, internal resolution between desired and accomplished goals, a good self-concept, general happiness, optimistic mood, and spontaneity. Other ingredients in the mix of life satisfaction may be physical comfort, financial security, productive activity, and an adequate social life.

The concept of life satisfaction can become an index of adjustment and well being. A satisfied person is generally happy and optimistic, relishes life, and has high perseverance, a sense of accomplishment, and a strong self-concept. Symptoms of low life satisfaction include: apathy, a sense of uselessness, and pessimism. Clearly, some retirees exhibit these later traits.

Life Satisfaction and Retirement

What has life satisfaction to do with retirement? Retirement planners formerly believed that if people were happy in their work, they would not want to risk a change by retiring; rather, they would prefer to continue working. As more data has been assessed, however, it has become clear that those who are satisfied with their life before retirement will probably move smoothly into retirement years and find satisfaction there as well, because they learned how to adjust to life's vicissitudes along the way.

The opposite is true as well. If our life satisfaction is currently low, our self-appraisal and overall satisfaction with life will not change radically in a positive direction as a result of our retirement. With comprehensive planning and adequate care of self, however, we can grow into a happy and successful retirement life phase.

A useful way of understanding life structure is to view our life as functioning in six "life arenas" (see Appendix Two):

1. Career or (ministry): our work life "life cause"
2. Family: our relationships with nuclear and extended family members

3. Relationships: our level of sharing of ourselves with others
4. Self: how we view our body; our overall self-esteem
5. Spirituality: our relationship with God
6. Leisure: what we do when we don't have to do anything else

Gauging our level of life satisfaction is really quite simple. All we have to do is rate each of the six life arenas in our life according to how satisfied we feel right now in that area. Rating each arena on a scale from one to ten, with one indicating "very low level of satisfaction" and ten indicating "maximum level of satisfaction," will produce a simple profile of the degree of contentment we feel in life right now.

The famous Jesuit author John Powell liked to say that happiness is an inside job (*Happiness Is an Inside Job*, Tabor Publishing, Dallas, Texas, 1989). Happiness can be defined as the degree to which we experience a sense of delight, fulfillment, pleasure, contentment, and Christ's presence in each of the six life arenas. Happiness emerges in us as a result of our own internal appraisal of how well our life is going now. Happiness includes such concepts as optimism, spontaneity, zest, stamina, perseverance, and accomplishments, to mention but a few. The opposite of happiness, unhappiness includes such negatives a apathy, resignation, helplessness, low self-esteem, and pessimism. We are the author of our current level of happiness—and this level of happiness is a good yardstick of how we will inject happiness into our life after we fully retire. That's why it pays big dividends to look closely at our current level of happiness as a means of gauging what areas are providing us happiness and what areas might demand some type of change in the future.

I've seen many persons in the preretirement stage of life just pining for the time when they could retire; they just couldn't wait. When I would ask these people why they wanted to retire, they didn't display any clear plans. Rather, I heard them express a simple desire to vacate the intolerable job they currently held. Their motivation for retiring was not to embrace a new lifestyle, but to vacate the lifestyle they were currently tolerating.

Let's consider the life of Margarete. She was the manager of a food-service kitchen that served hundreds of meals every day. She had full responsibility of the total operation: ordering food, preparing meals, supervising the preparation, displaying and distributing meals, collecting money. Margarete did a good job and, while she wasn't clicking her heels in delight over her job, she had mastered it and was comfortable in it. Certainly, there were days that were better than others, but overall she was adequately satisfied with her career.

Margarete, however, was not satisfied with the area of her life that included relationships. She was a widow, having nursed her husband the last years of his life. He had died four years ago and Margarete was lonely. She had appropriately mourned for her husband, and gradually grew to believe that she needed another life partner. This she wanted more than anything else. Yet potential partners were not easy to come by. Margarete did everything she could to find a compatible "someone," but her efforts remained unrewarded. Eventually, she began thinking that her job was the reason she couldn't seem to find success in relationships. As this idea pressed in on her thinking, she became obsessed with the idea that she had to get out of her job just as soon as she could.

Within three months Margarete "retired." Unfortunately, the bliss that she hoped for in her retirement didn't materialize. Instead, Margarete faced the same dilemma in retirement that she faced before retirement. Retiring from our work arena in an attempt to rectify another unhappy life arena is probably not the ideal way to start a new retirement lifestyle.

Margarete's story is the story of many people who find themselves in their new retirement lifestyle, still faced with the same levels of life dissatisfaction they experienced before they retired. Retirement doesn't "fix" life; it very rarely takes us "off the hook," and it almost never makes us "new" persons. The person I take into my retirement is the same one that I've been living with all along.

This all points to the same conclusion: we need more than financial planning for our retirement stage of life. We need to look deeply into ourselves and assess our current level of happiness. Whatever level of happiness we find there is what we have created and what we developed on our own. Regardless of the life situation in which we find ourselves, we have to keep in mind that we decide how happy we will be. Using our retirement as the outside means of getting us out of ourselves, of somehow removing any discouragement we feel in the depths of our being, is not only misguided, it's doomed to make us feel even worse.

Retirement As a Spiritual Journey

Healthy resolution of this sixth retirement success factor rests upon our relationship with God. It requires a genuine appreciation that God truly loves us, and that God wants the best for us. This means that we must listen deeply inside and discern how the Holy Spirit is nudging us and in what direction. In this way we become more sensitive to the light of God working in our lives. We awaken to the grace of God and become evermore sensitive to experiencing God's grace.

Retirement challenges us to listen to the sounds of our souls. What are these sounds? What do they mean for us? We learn to see the flashes of God's love everywhere and to open ourselves more fully to the power of patience, trust, faith, stamina, and steadfastness.

Real happiness emerges as we awaken to the love and beauty that exist right in our own midst. Genuine satisfaction with our life emerges when we can arise from that spiritual slumber which previously left us unsure of the meaning of our lives. The monetary gain that the world claims to be the purpose of retirement leads to: living an anemic rather than a robust life of vitality; a withering of our own life force; and an erosion of our dreams. Ultimately, listening to only the world's answer to retirement leads to a consumption of our very selves rather than an extension and an expression of who we are.

Wholeness vs. Fragmentation

Wholeness is the grace-power of this sixth retirement success factor. Wholeness speaks to our sense of integrity, that is, being intact, complete, and undivided. Practicing wholeness means concentrating our efforts toward one goal. Wholeness is a spiritual concept indicating a unity with God; a sense of togetherness exists. The opposite of wholeness is fragmentation.

Fragmentation is the opposite of wholeness. When we are fragmented we are broken, disjointed, unconnected. Our various component parts are not "glued together"; we lack cohesiveness, we are not operating in unity. When we are fragmented we work against ourselves.

Affirmation

Lord, grant that I may find zest, delight, and optimism all the years of my life. Let me see that retirement affords me a new start from which I can build a new life structure in all the arenas of my life. Help me to look deeply into myself and find the glorious happiness that You, dear Lord, have left there waiting for me all along. Help me to remove any discouragements that may be inhibiting my expression of the joy and good cheer You have invested in me. Help me appreciate the simple abundance that is my inheritance from You. Help me awaken to the love and beauty that surrounds me.

CHAPTER 7

Have Dreams

*If the physician is concerned about
fostering (creating) false hope,
he should be no less concerned about
fostering (creating) false fears and false despair.*

NORMAN COUSINS

Retirement Success Pearl #7

Future Quality of Life: The degree to which you have
dreams and can foresee life satisfaction and happiness
for yourself in your next stage of life.

Retirement Challenge #7: How can I develop and maintain hope in the future?

Your Need for Dreams: Jan and Her Insecure Future

Jan was astonished. She sat with her husband listening to the human-resources representative of the company where her husband, Tom, had worked for more than twenty-five years; Tom was accepting an early retirement package. To use the word "accepting" is actually misleading. Tom would be involuntarily terminated without a "retirement package" if he did not "voluntarily" accept what was offered. Jan and Tom felt forced into taking the retirement package.

Even though Jan was naturally aggravated and frustrated, she accepted the fact that Tom was indeed retiring. She felt unsure about what was ahead, but she was resigned to it. She was astonished, however, by what she heard the human-resources representative say: Tom had no funds in the company 401(k) individual pension plan, because he had never contributed to it. All he had was the small severance package that the company was offering and his normal company pension which, while nice, was insufficient for them to live on. Since Tom was only fifty-eight years old, he would have to wait at least four years before he was eligible to begin drawing social security.

Jan was furious! All these years Tom had assured her that they didn't have to worry about retirement, that he had made sure that they would have enough to live on. She had interpreted this to mean that he was contributing monthly to the 401(k) plan. Now there was nothing! Jan was flabbergasted! How could Tom do this to her? She felt betrayed, abandoned and, for the first time since retirement had become part of her immediate future, scared. Strangely enough, her fear was not from the reduction of money; Jan was a nurse and she could continue in her position as long as she liked. No, she was scared because this had injected an entirely new feeling of insecurity about the future. She realized that the security she had felt for so many years was simply a myth, an illusion; it wasn't based on anything. She felt that she couldn't rely on Tom, certainly not like she had in the past. The future looked insecure to Jan; it no longer offered her a solid footing as it had in the past. She felt emotionally shaky and imbalanced.

Life Satisfaction—Projected

Satisfaction with our current life is not entirely defined by surveying only our current lifestyle. Life satisfaction, or happiness, takes on a vitally more functional dimension when the notion is projected into the future. What do we see for our life "down the road"? At our core we naturally look to the future. A hopeful future motivates us to wish and even expect that what is to come will bestow on us gifts of its own. Our projected life satisfaction, that is, what we believe our future years will bring, becomes another barometer of our positive disposition about our retirement years and an accurate indicator of finding personal success therein.

In the last chapter we measured our current life satisfaction. In this chapter we'll look at life satisfaction through the lens of the future. Measuring both current and projected life satisfaction together is a means of evaluating our readiness to secure a place of harmony and happiness in retirement. This leads us once again to look at our life structure, that is, what makes up our life?

Six Life Arenas

As we did in the last chapter, we find a useful way of understanding life structure by viewing our life as functioning in six life arenas:

1. *Career or (ministry):* our work life "life cause"
2. *Family:* our relationships with nuclear and extended family members

3. *Relationships*: our level of sharing of ourselves with others
4. *Self*: how we view our body; our overall self-esteem
5. *Spirituality*: our relationship with God
6. *Leisure*: what we do when we don't have to do anything else

As we did in the last chapter, we gauge our level of life satisfaction in each of the six arenas. We rate each of the six life arenas according to how satisfied we *believe that we will feel in the future*, rating each on a scale from one to ten, with one indicating "very low level of satisfaction" and ten indicating "maximum level of satisfaction." Once again, we will produce a simple profile of the degree of contentment we feel about our life in the future. (You may want to compare your rating in the last chapter to your ratings in this chapter. Do you see more life satisfaction for yourself "now," in the present, or do you project more life satisfaction for yourself in your next life stage?)

Projected life satisfaction is somewhat difficult to measure quantitatively. However, we can "get a fix" on it by simply writing one retirement goal for ourselves in each of the six life arenas. The result will be an elementary blueprint of how we would like our life to proceed and grow in the future. If we want to be more complete, we can write goals in each of the six life arenas, first projecting out five years, then ten years, fifteen years, and so on. This exercise is not a dismal demonstration of demise, but rather an invigorating self-instruction of planning. When we have a clearer understanding of the future, we will find our present life more meaningful.

Projected quality of life in the future is a clear retirement success factor because what we expect to happen, what we "see" will probably happen, what we project to happen—probably will. It's called a self-fulfilling prophecy: what we see for ourselves will, all other things being equal, more than likely actually happen. Now if we project that we will win the state lottery in the future, this might be somewhat outside the boundaries of reality. But more often than not our future projections, our goals, seem to come with self-guidance systems prepackaged inside. They seem to have their own homing devices that put our projections on automatic pilot. We automatically begin arranging our life around that which we firmly envision for ourselves in the future and, little by little, the goal begins to materialize. All along we have been subconsciously engineering our life to make room for this goal and to lead rather logically to the end point of the goal. The old adage, "Watch what you ask for, because you just might get it" seems to have particular relevance here.

Hope

Our sense of life satisfaction today requires that we have a sense of a positive future. When we project into the future with joy, delight, fulfillment, and contentment, we tend to look forward to a time of personal meaning and purpose. This all adds up to hope. When we lose hope, we develop a nagging doubt that happiness will not last. We, like Jan, develop fears about tomorrow, that it may not be as rewarding as today. Without hope, we feel our desires for a better life tomorrow being dashed. In short, when we lose hope we find fear.

Hope is the spiritual confidence, assurance, and security that all will be well. Hope gives us the absolute reassurance that God truly *is* in charge. Hope means that we understand that God's plan for us is unfolding as it should. Hope helps us come to realize that nothing in this world can derail the momentum of God.

Hope brings the promise of fairness, goodness, and cheer. Cheer comes from knowing that the "right" and "might" of God are perennial. God's love always blooms again in the spiritual springtime. Hope helps us believe that the Holy Spirit eventually brings more good than "bad" from any situation. This all happens in God's way and in God's time.

Hope enables us to believe that love will remain the compelling force in the universe, and in our lives. Hope tells us that there is no power mighty enough to topple God. Hope allows us the perfect expectation that God's will prevails. Hope gives us spiritual optimism and hopeful enthusiasm. Hope gives cheer in a landscape that otherwise seems somewhat inhospitable at times.

Integrity vs. Despair

Erik Erikson was probably the most renowned adult developmentalist of this century. He proposed that we go through seven stages of development in our lifetime, the final stage being "integrity vs. despair." Integrity is that psychological "place" from which we can see our entire life and can make the judgment that our life has been "good." Certainly, we might want to make a few changes but, all in all, the choices we made and the challenges we took on were "good." This sense of integrity, says Erikson, is commonly developed in the later years, as we grow in wisdom. People who do not or cannot develop integrity are at risk for lapsing into despair. Despair is the condition where hope seems to be lost.

Too many retirees suffer from a loss of integrity and the consequent loss of hope. When this occurs, retirees run the risk of becoming despondent. They lose their will to live to the fullest. Without integrity and hope they feel themselves being cleaved from life. They forget that they are children of God, and they founder in worry and anxiety. They grow to dread life. Jan is entering the outer reaches of this unfortunate condition of agitation and questioning.

When we cannot come to personal integration, our expectations for the future are necessarily clouded. While our attitudes reflect a lackluster quality of dismay, our world becomes emotional isolated and spiritually stark.

Like Saint Monica's hope for her son, Augustine, we harbor

and safeguard hope that our own waywardness, our own broken-ness, will someday find healing. We all need a "future"; we all need tomorrow so that today has meaning and purpose. When we are relatively sure that tomorrow will be "good,"we go a long way toward realizing the self-fulfilling prophecy goal.

Affirmation

Lord, help me construct positive and growthful images in my mind about what my retirement will be for me. I know that my thoughts seek expression. Whatever my mind truly locks onto when it is connected to You, will bring me happiness beyond anything that I could have conceived of on my own. Lord, I shall do whatever I can to open myself to the fantastic power of Your hope. I know that hope lights the way to happiness, and hope gives me the surety and security to live in peace; even as I walk the mystery of this life. Even though tomorrow is unknown to me today, I do know that You will be there with me in my future as You are with me today. It is this assurance that propels me to make life decisions today in the confidence of Your power and abiding presence.

CHAPTER 8

Construct Purpose

Ever more people today have the means to live,
but no meaning to live for.

VIKTOR FRANKL

Retirement Success Pearl #8

Spirituality and Meaning: The degree to which you have
found, and can actually implement, a sense of personal
life purpose, a cause, that allows you to connect better
with yourself and with God.

Retirement Challenge #8: How can I find purpose and
personal meaning in my retirement years?

The Need to Construct Purpose: Sissy's Dream

Sissy sank down into the hassock with a weary sigh; it had been a long day at the fabric shop. She had spent the entire day on her feet, talking with customers, helping them with their sewing projects, and giving them her sought-after advice on assorted topics related to interior design.

Sissy had been working at the fabric shop for more than four years, ever since her husband's retirement from the auto assembly plant where he had worked for thirty years. She liked her work and enjoyed the people and the creative side of it all: redesigning patterns, choosing colors and fabrics, coordinating soft and hard accessories for home decoration, and the like. She was an art major for the two years she attended college, and had taken several art courses at the local community college. Sissy subscribed to several home design and interior design periodicals, and even liked reading *Architectural Digest*. There seemed no end to the depth of the field she had adopted as her own. She never tired of learning more about it.

As much as she liked the field of her work, Sissy especially enjoyed people. Over time she had become more than a shop clerk or a design consultant to her customers. Many of them had grown to respect Sissy as a friend, even a mentor.

Sissy was a woman of faith and, without being obviously evangelistic, she was able to give testimony of her faith in many small ways. She was becoming increasing awake to God's power in her life. When she and a customer would be hunched over a bolt of fabric, paging through a wallpaper catalog, or viewing a new print or painting together, Sissy would realize that she was sharing more than design advice. She became aware that the customer was sharing something of personal import, searching for connection with Sissy. As customers got to know Sissy they instinctively were drawn to her peace, her gentle confidence, and her luminous and generous personality. Sissy was beginning to realize and to "own" the fact that people saw her as a woman of stature, a woman who was comfortable with herself, a woman could enjoyed the moment as a piece of the glory that is God. This gave her an immense feeling of goodwill and a strange kind of spiritual intimacy, not only with the customer but with the whole world. She was seeing herself and her place in God's world differently—and it was glorious.

Sissy had raised six children and now had nine grandchildren. She loved her family and always looked forward to their visits. She loved keeping up with the many events and items of personal interest that emerged from the families that had spun off from her own. She especially connected with her daughters and daughters-in-law, treating each with dignity.

Sissy remembered well her own early years of marriage, with young children, and the stress of loving she experienced. She knew the young women in her life felt the same things, and she was eager to support them in any way she could. She loved her sons and sons-in-law too, but she felt a special mission when it came to her daughters and daughters-in-law. Often times Sissy would muse that this was a good life; certainly not the retirement lifestyle she had anticipated, but one that was unquestionably worth living. Life was good!

Life Meaning

The late Viktor Frankl, the noted Jewish psychiatrist who witnessed the death of his own family in the Nazi concentration camps of World War II, tells us that in order for our life to be authentic, it must become a journey of meaning.

Retirement gives us the forum in which our search for meaning can play out in ways only dreamed about in our former lifestyle. Retirement is pregnant with meaning potential. It is this very quest for increasing meaning that provides the vehicle for us to drive ever deeper into our own spiritual abundance.

Those who venture into retirement unenlightened, risk their new and undefined lifestyle becoming a challenge to their self-esteem, rather than realizing it as the life-enhancer and self-affirmer they had supposed it would be. They risk entering into a life that is anemic of meaning and faint of purpose, a life where personal worth seems uncertain, a life where yesterday seems so full and life-giving as compared to the emptiness of today.

Retirement calls for a shift in the way we perceive and experience life itself. This shift is away from a simple quantitative perspective, and toward an increasingly qualitative vision. This shift perforce brings changes in our values. Such a shift in our view of personal and life meaning is not easy to do.

We are unconsciously, yet so powerfully, influenced by our culture. From every corner of our commercial culture we are bombarded by mistaken notions telling us that the pursuit of worldly pleasures is the norm in retirement. Yet a retirement lifestyle made of such fabric quickly unravels. Spirituality, our search for meaning, weaves a cloth of rich color and lasting quality. It robes us with an invigorated strength of purpose, an ascending consciousness of self, and an expanded appreciation for the endeavors of retirement living.

Life Purpose

"Meaning" is something that we experience; it is a felt sense. We *feel* meaning. Meaning can be described in many ways: as a feeling of warmth and goodness; a feeling of goodwill and giving; a feeling of fulfillment that pushes aside the more shadowy aspects of this world; a feeling of well-being and security; a feeling of connection with God; a feeling of intimacy by being a part of peace-making and justice-building. This list of descriptors could go on. Yet, what is it that offers us these wonderful feelings? What do we need to do to feel the psychological and emotional satisfaction that only meaning offers?

Meaning comes from one thing and one thing only: the pursuing of a *purpose* that is larger than ourselves. Purpose is personal. Sissy's purpose, for example, was many faceted: connecting with her customers on more than a mercantile basis; interacting with her children and grandchildren; caring for her husband and helping him manage his diabetes. Yet, when these life tasks are distilled to their bare essential, Sissy's purpose could be stated simply as "offering herself to others in God's light." This simple statement becomes the primary motivational force in Sissy's life. It is from this that magnificent meaning flows into Sissy's heart. As a consequence, Sissy feels fulfilled and complete. She feels herself.

Purpose is that one goal, dream, life-cause, mission, quest, or life-drive that stimulates our creativity, clarifies our direction, enlists our unique talents and gifts, ignites our soul, and invigorates our spirit. When we are living "on purpose," our health improves, our mind is clearer, and our spirituality is enhanced. Our overall level of life satisfaction in each of our six life arenas is working together in synergistic harmony; we are "in sync."

This condition is sometimes called "flow." Flow is when we become engrossed in the process of what we are doing to the point that it becomes our "being." Flow takes our complete attention; there are no distractions at that moment, no competing irritations. Living "on purpose" is a life condition that gives less meaning to the everyday issues of time, material possessions, personal achievements, and self-esteem, and gives greater meaning to the more transcendent conditions of connection with others, communion with God, and fostering the common good of all.

Each of us must have a goal, a cause, a mission, a burning desire that fills us. Life goals or purpose stimulate our inner treasure, the depository of God's promise of abundance. Living "on purpose" gives rise to wellness and activates those marvelous healing powers right inside of us. Purpose lights our way in this world and keeps us focused on God, on the most noble parts of others and of ourselves. Purpose fills us with zest, vitality, and youthfulness.

Our world lacks no problems. Nor does our world lack any talent. We have an abundance of problems and we have an abundance of talent. What may be missing—especially for those retirees who listen to the worldly siren song telling them that pursuit of the pleasure principle is the objective of retirement—are the very things that give life to life. Among these are:

- *Vision* to see the problems of our culture as potential life goals that are rich with potential personal purpose.
- *Perseverance* to take on such cultural and societal problems as our own personal cause.
- *Strength* to pursue even one of these problems as our personal mission.
- *Passion* to embrace a community problem with that burning desire that fires the heart.

Christ gave each of us a goal, a cause, a burning desire, a spiritual dream, that is uniquely ours. The retirement phase of life, the wonderful time of personal renewal, is that time when we can delve deeply within ourselves and unearth what God has in mind for us. God gave us the vineyards: the highways and byways of the countryside, the corners and cul-de-sacs of the suburbs, the back streets and alleys of the cities, the sidewalks and gutters of the metropolis. There we find God's children in need; there we find the poverty of human existence; there we find the problems in abundance; there we find purpose, that glorious purpose that offers us the most magnificent meaning this side of heaven.

Christ shows us how to take up the cross, and we are charged to do no less. The current worldly attitude about retirement obscures the true mission and purpose of our journey here on this earth. Make no mistake about it: we are called each and every day to take up the social causes of peace and justice, the human causes of care and compassion, and the spiritual causes of prayer and reflection.

Pathways of Change

What pathways may be followed to ensure that retirement does not become a retreat from the world, a refusal to participate, a shutting down of our interest and involvement in living and loving? How can we counter the confusion that retirement may bring to our very being, a confusion that may cause us to mistake our new lifestyle as useless, which in turn leaves life meaningless? How can we respond to retirement and not simply react to it?

To approach our true self in retirement, we need to clearly identify the meaning we are striving to fulfill. We need to pursue self-transcendence of our simple human dimensions and take on a vastly more robust sense of self made up of those celestial components within us that are beyond ourselves.

The changes that retirement brings can either arrest our psycho-spiritual development or propel us to new personal discoveries of our self and a fresh personality reorganization. Our work can become for us a good place to hide from our own fears, a veil over our vision blinding us from our true purpose here, a block to our essential spirituality. In retirement, however, we face ourselves without the encumbrance of our work; we look deeply into ourselves and find either fear and pain or the source of all positive power.

In retirement we are confronted, perhaps for the first time, with those fears that we might have squirreled away in the niches of our mind. These fears can serve as an empty cup, allowing us to dip deeply into our spiritual reservoir of strength, hope, and faith.

Retirement asks that we listen within our heart and soul, and in so doing, we challenge the action-based pursuits of the ego. Our ego is constantly pushing us to look outward, outside of ourselves to find satisfaction. Our ego continuously urges us for more, more, more things. Our ego sometimes whispers in our inner ear, and sometimes screams at us to *do* this or to *do* that. Such frenetic searching for satisfaction outside ourselves neglects the needs of the interior soul; it drowns out the internal nudges of our Spirit, our True Self, and renders us imbalanced.

The emerging wisdom in the retirement years refers to our discernment and judgment. This wisdom includes experience not only of an interior nature, but of the wider world as well. It is this balance between the interior and external world, sometimes absent in our working years, that can come to flower in retirement and allow us to view or quest for meaning more comprehensively. Our search for peace and justice is a search in both dimensions of our lives. It allows us to understand more fully Christ's admonition, that we are *in* the world, but not *of* it.

Our Own Spirituality—the Center of Our Meaning

Our own spirituality can become the centerpiece of advancing meaning in retirement. Retirement is first a transition in spirituality, followed by a shift in our psychosocial, ministerial, or financial condition.

Advancing spirituality as the motivating force for meaning enhancement requires that we modify the self, rather than the world, as our primary site for change. Here is the elegant solution for growth and development in retirement living. Our spirituality nudges us to seek change first in our interior world, rather than the external one. This means relinquishing the achievement-oriented mentality of our younger years in favor of an internal focus for change.

Inspiration vs. Lifelessness

Inspiration is the grace-filled power that guides us toward our true purpose and hence to the outer edges of personal meaning throughout our life. Inspiration means that we become infused with light, life, and the knowledge of being guided by the Divine. The spiritual reality within us has been touched. The consequence of the lack of inspiration in our lives is the harrowing sense of numbness we call being lifelessness.

Lifelessness means that the forces of life and light within us have been covered over. The Spirit is always there, yet when we become lifeless, we fail to listen, when we fail to see the flow of love in our world.

Affirmation

Lord, help me find new purpose. Now that making a living is no longer clouding my way, I am free to delve deeply into the depth of my soul and discover the dream that You, dear Lord, have placed there eons ago. My purpose is as unique as my fingerprint. Help me shift my vision away from the busyness of the world and onto that which really counts. Some desire pulses through me, something much larger than my own needs is nudging me on. Grant me the vision to find the path to purpose, the perseverance to enter the path, and the strength to pursue the path of purpose. Help me find the passion of my life, dear Lord; help me see where I can reflect Your light onto at least one of the world's problems. Help me give of myself to others so that I may receive the wonderful, warm feeling of living a meaningful life.

CHAPTER 9

Have Fun

To be for one day entirely at leisure is
to be for one day immortal.

CHINESE PROVERB

Retirement Success Pearl #9

Respect for Leisure: The degree you can have fun through personally satisfying endeavors that rejuvenate your body, and/or stimulate your mind, and/or enrich your soul.

Retirement Challenge #9: How can I find the means to rest my body, stimulate my mind, and enrich my soul in retirement?

∞

The Need to Have Fun: Ray's Retirement Illusion

As I walked into the television studio to be interviewed on the meaning of a "good" retirement, the studio manager said that she wanted me to meet Ray. "Ray?" I asked, "Who's Ray?" "He's our lead cameraman," she said. "He'll be retiring next week after almost thirty years with the station. Ray was our very first cameraman. He was here the day the station opened." "Well," I said, "I'll be glad to meet Ray."

Ray appeared several minutes later. He was a youngish looking man, slender, wearing jeans with a wide belt, a full head of hair he combed in a wave, with two little curls sweeping over his forehead. "Hello, Ray," I said. "I'm glad to meet you. I understand that this is your last week here at the studio. Next week you'll be retired." "Sure will," he responded. "This time next week the studio will be all but forgotten." "Tell me, Ray," I inquired, "What do you plan to do in your retirement?" "Me... I'm goin' fishin'!" he replied with something of a flip assertiveness.

What was Ray really telling me? Did he really think that he would go fishing 365 days a year, every year of his retirement? Was his response grounded in well-considered alternatives? Was it the outcome of a process of personal insight that befitted the length of time Ray was likely to spend in his retirement phase of life? Was this a genuine response, or was it simply something to say? Was this a "throw-away" response designed to cover up the possibility that Ray had not seriously considered the many options available to him? Could it be that Ray had not dug into himself and come up with his uniqueness, that specialness that defined him? Had Ray not discovered that unique direction of mission in his soul that would give him the marvelous and necessary sense of personal fulfillment we call life meaning? Did he not feel the ache inside that craved well-being? What did "goin' fishin'" mean to Ray? Did it suggest a potential path leading to personal fulfillment, or was it simply a statement of confusion,

giving testimony that Ray had no earthly idea what he planned
to do with the longest stage of his life: retirement?

Leisure

Leisure can be defined as "that which you do when you don't have
to do anything else." Each of us finds different satisfaction, contentment, and/or challenge in different activities. One person's leisure
can be another person's work. Yet leisure of some sort seems to be
a universal desire. In our retirement stage of development, unlike
previous life stages, leisure can become more central.

Six Categories of Leisure

Leisure can be divided into six different categories. Which of
these six do you seem to favor in your world?

1. *Social interaction:* Enjoying time with others, finding
   a sense of satisfaction and even personal fulfillment in
   participating with friends, acquaintances, parishioners,
   community members, etc.
2. *Spectator appreciation:* Drawing stimulation from
   watching things outside oneself. These can range from
   spectator sports, traveling, "people watching," or watching nature in its various forms.
3. *Creative expression:* Finding solace, peace, fulfillment,
   and satisfaction in expressing oneself in some form,
   such as painting, writing, photography, various crafts,
   performing arts, and so on.
4. *Mental stimulation:* Finding interest and invigoration of
   the mind in any of many forms of intellectual stimulation,
   such as reading, going to museums, attending lectures,
   collecting something, keeping abreast of current events,
   and so on.

5. *Physical exercise:* Finding an internal sense of relaxation and even spiritual centeredness in various forms of physical activity, such as participatory sports and yoga. Any form of bodily exercise that brings health and an internal sense of well-being fits into this category.

6. *Solitary relaxation:* Finding peace, relaxation for the body, and stimulation for the mind in solitary activities. Reading, listening to music, day dreaming, loafing, taking a nap, all fit into this category.

Leisure: A Fundamental Need

Leisure is one of our fundamental needs. If we push ourselves too far for too long without stopping for rest, we are asking for a gradual erosion of our human spirit. Leisure is powerful; it has the energy to reconstruct us, to reconstitute us, to reconnect us, to our central core. Like any other human need, the human need for leisure is varied; some people need more leisure than others. Some people need more rest, more food, more exercise, more vitamin C, more stimulation, more nurture (TLC) than do others. Leisure is the same; the need for leisure seems to be as unevenly distributed in the population as are all other human traits.

Experts in creativity, that is, persons who study how the mind works most effectively, have discovered that frequent and regular breaks away from our primary activity actually foster increased creativity and productivity, rather than the opposite. Leisure offers this well of refreshment that seems to clear the cobwebs from our minds and allows us to think more clearly. Retirees do need to see leisure as a valuable human endeavor; they need to recognize their leisure needs and act on them.

The very idea of a vacation connotes a break from the routine of our everyday routine. The word *vacation* comes from the root word *vacate*, which means to "go away from." If we are to remain focused on the core issues of our lives, we must periodically "vacate" our routines. We must go away from, digress, divert our attention onto something or someone else. It doesn't matter what the diversion is; one leisure activity is not inherently better than another for producing diversion. It all boils down to a matter of personal taste.

"Perhaps it is most helpful," says the late Dr. Harold Riker, former professor at the University of Florida, "to think of leisure in terms of, first, an attitude of mind and, second, what it can do for an individual rather than what it is. An important point is that leisure must be conceptualized in much the same way as work. Like work, leisure can be the means for developing feelings of self-worth, social status, and one's individual potential. Leisure too can lead to self-discovery and a better quality of life."

This view of leisure as a means of personal growth and development is central to the retirement experience. This developmental perspective is echoed by leisure consultant Dr. Joanne Minnihan who maintains that there are five major leisure needs:

1. Improve physical health: Increase strength and endurance, improve circulation, maintain coordination
2. Enhance emotional well-being: Ventilate or escape stress, share oneself, relax one's mind and body, improve self-confidence
3. Enrich mental well-being: Maintain clear thinking, improve creativity, make own decisions, maintain memory
4. Expand social needs: Social participation, improve trust, allow others to feel important, empathy, build rapport
5. Find meaningful roles in life: Make important contributions to society, positively change life, being of service to others

The key element in finding success in our leisure, points out Dr. Minnihan, is self-motivation; we must want to satisfy our leisure needs. So what motivates us to embrace leisure as a source of human enrichment and expansion rather than as a waste of time, as our deeply ingrained work ethic would pushes us to do? What helps us see leisure as, indeed, ordained by Christ?

To get a view of how your leisure activities affect you, place a check next to any of the following that may describe aspects of you in your understanding of leisure:

____ motivation
____ recognition
____ socialization
____ meaningful role
____ decision making
____ develop interests and skills
____ intellectual stimulation
____ creativity and self-expression
____ self-confidence
____ exercise
____ relaxation
____ entertainment
____ reality awareness
____ substitute for past work roles

Positive living in retirement means adequate recognition and implementation of our leisure needs. Leisure is not the only factor contributing to retirement success, of course, but it is among the most powerful of all fifteen factors and can spell doom or boom for us in our retirement years. Keep in mind that those who register the highest life satisfaction in their later years are those forward-looking persons who have already generated specific leisure interests and who pursue them with gusto.

The Spirituality of Leisure

Quality leisure reminds us that our sole purpose in life is not to *do* but to *be.* As such, leisure becomes a condition of the soul in that it helps build wholeness. I know a priest in our nation's capitol who weekly vacates his role as provincial of his order and spends one night at a homeless shelter. There his identity as a priest is hidden; he is simply a man. In that capacity he interacts with the men who come for assistance. He simply talks with them, listens to them, tries to enjoy them—nothing more. This is his leisure. He claims that when he drives home from the shelter in the early morning, after very little or no sleep, the feeling of personal meaning is simply awesome. Something touches his soul at that shelter; it's a something that he doesn't experience in his regular day-to-day job.

Leisure also includes a contemplative mode of internal perception. Leisure helps us look inward and find the childlike qualities that have always been there but may have gotten covered over. Where, for example, and in what situations do we experience the childlike quality of awe? or delight? or wonder? When we have that experience, we are experiencing the spirit side of leisure. Leisure helps us see God's creations for what they are, right now in the present. Leisure helps us appreciate the wonderful "now" of God. Sr. Marie Therese Ruthmann says that "celebration of things as they are is the soul of leisure."

Leisure is wherever we find our well of spiritual refreshment: in a sunset, a moon beam, children playing on a playground, sunlight dancing on the kitchen table, at liturgy, Communion, wherever. We seek those places that touch the miraculous spot in our inner core which is the residence of our changeless God within us.

Indeed, life without leisure creates a bleak psychological and spiritual landscape. Life without leisure becomes anemic. On a spiritual level, leisure connects us to our life purpose. Leisure can provide us with meaningful roles, opportunities for making important contributions, potentials to transform lifestyles, and the capacity to serve others.

Unhealthy resolution of this ninth retirement success factor bodes ill for us in our middle and later years. It means that we find it difficult to reflect on the meaning of our lives. Our lives degenerate in a routine of "doing things" rather than a mix of activities that include just being appreciative of who we are and how we have been gifted. We may ultimately become callous, anxious, and self-absorbed. On the other hand, successfully developing a leisurely lifestyle in retirement gives us that wonderful pause to be grateful. Brother David Stendl Rast says it well when he says: "Who among us wouldn't give our right arm for a grateful heart?" When we can truly fold leisure into the sumptuous soup of our life, we find the heavenly taste of serenity.

Jesus encourages leisure. He is a model of retreating for rest to commune with the Father. Many times he simply wanders away from the crowds and the bustle of his ministry to seek solace. Indeed, the only specific reference to the word *leisure* in the New Testament is in Mark 6:30–32: "The apostles returned to Jesus, and told him all that they had done and taught. And he said to them, 'Come away to a deserted place all by yourselves and rest a while.' For many were coming and going, and they had no leisure even to eat. And they went away in the boat to a deserted place by themselves."

Leisure and Retirement

There seems no question that leisure commands a more central focus in the lives of retirees. Some retirees even believe that retirement and leisure are synonymous. In all probably, the manner, style, and intensity of leisure are different in retirement than they have been in our entire life. Yet, even though the importance of leisure is certainly raised in our retirement stage, we must be careful not to raise it so high that it occupies *the* central focus of our life. For when and if leisure does become the primary goal around which our whole life revolves, we are inadvertently doing damage to our very souls. As retirees we certainly can pursue a *leisurely* lifestyle, but beware of pursuing a *leisure* lifestyle. This was the mistake that Ray was about to make.

Leisure is always a diversion; it takes us away from our central focus of living. Leisure gives us rest and recuperation from the rigors and the potential monotony of our ordinary life, not because our main focus in life is drudgery, but because we want and apparently need a break so that we can be even more focused on our central life task. When leisure becomes our central life task, however, it ceases to be leisure, because it is no longer diversionary.

This is the paradox of leisure. Leisure must be diversionary to remain leisure. Pursuing a leisure lifestyle is impossible, for the moment it becomes the main focus of life it isn't leisure any more. This is why we are to pursue a *leisurely* lifestyle, not a *leisure* lifestyle. When leisure becomes the main thrust of our life, it ceases to bring us the harvest of benefit that it formerly did. We then need to develop another leisure endeavor to provide us with diversion from our new life task, which was formerly only a leisure endeavor.

This distinction between leisure and our life mission, which we discussed in the last chapter, is more than simple semantics; this distinction is quite real. If Ray actually does try to make fishing his central life task, how long do you think it will be before Ray becomes bored with fishing and begins looking at it as just another task to perform, seeing fishing the same way he formerly looked at his job? How long will it be until fishing loses the diversionary quality it formerly provided for Ray and simply becomes another thing to do? Fishing will no longer offer him rejuvenation for the body, stimulation for the mind, and enrichment for the soul.

Making leisure the central forum of our retirement lives only ensures that we disembowel the very source of the gifts that leisure has to offer us. Leisure loses its luster when we let it take center stage in our lives. Like a vacation spot that loses its appeal when we actually move there, thinking that life will be great when we can make our leisure activity our central life activity only leads to disappointment.

Joy vs. Dejection

The power—grace, really—that fires our path toward healthy leisure is joy. Joy refers to our ability of expressing pleasure or delight in celebration. Joy is the unspoken, inner result of knowing God is our true reality, and the emotional response of feeling God's grace sustaining us. The opposite of joy is dejection.

When we are dejected, we are gloomy, downcast, dismal, and melancholy. Dejection separates us from God in that it clouds over the joy in our hearts; we brood, sulk, and find little cheer in our world. Dejection makes critics out of us.

Affirmation

Let me truly value leisure, dear Lord. Help me to place leisure in its proper context in my retirement; not to either undervalue it nor overvalue it. Help me to see the power in leisure, to find the elegant satisfactions and the wonderful delights that are resident in leisure for me. Grant me new vision, Lord, so that I may see the full potential of leisure for me. Let me not fall into the blindness of only seeing leisure as rest or play; while leisure is certainly that, it is also an opportunity for important contributions, a time for enhanced meaning in life, and also a time for becoming more profoundly acquainted with the most noble parts of myself. Let me understand that leisure is also a condition of my soul which includes contemplative aspects just as much as "doing" aspects. Leisure is one of my wells where I can go for spiritual refreshment, as well as another arena for spiritual delight. Help me to recognize that leisure is only my diversion from the central thrust of my retirement living.

CHAPTER 10

Welcome Change

*Life inflicts the same setbacks and tragedies on the optimist
as on the pessimist, but the optimist weathers them better. The
optimist bounces back from defeat, and,
with his life somewhat poorer, he picks up and starts again.
The pessimist gives up and falls into depression.*

MARTIN SELIGMAN

Retirement Success Pearl #10

Personal Flexibility: The degree that you can welcome change into your life and can consciously adapt to changes outside yourself by making modifications within yourself.

Retirement Challenge #10: How can I remain fully open to new growth and personal development on all levels in my retirement years?

81

Ability to Welcome Change: Phyllis's New Life

Phyllis was, once again, sitting in the emergency waiting room. Unfortunately Phyllis was becoming a regular; she was on a first-name basis with some of the staff. This was the third time in two weeks that she was forced to bring her thirty-five-year-old son for emergency treatment. Her son, Randy, suffered from epilepsy, along with other assorted disorders. His medical picture was muddy at best; one chronic ailment would abate while another seemed to flare. Keeping some sort of medical balance seemed all but impossible for Randy. One ailment only served to complicate the others, and visa versa. This was not a new condition, but clearly it was a worsening one.

Phyllis had been a nurse. She had worked at the hospital for many years before she retired three years ago at the age of sixty-five. Her dreams for the retirement lifestyle she hoped for were all "on hold"—for now. She was exasperated, tired, confused, drained. Most of all Phyllis was scared of what might become of her son and, by extension, of what might become of the retirement she would like to live. Randy can't drive; his epilepsy prevents it. His medications cloud his mind, so that he has trouble holding down even low-stress jobs. Randy has never been married—his medical problems have always mitigated against a long-term relationship.

Phyllis felt stuck, blocked from making her own decisions, and thwarted by the immense problem she now encountered. Would she simply have to resign herself to being a full-time care provider for the remainder of her years? Was this to be "the rest of her life"?

Phyllis was an active person. She had a reputation as a positively motivated person, always with a strong "can-do" spirit. She was always ready to tackle anything. She had good training; her father died when she was only five years old, and she had to be the big sister to her three younger siblings while her mother worked six days a week. At a young age Phyllis learned the meaning of responsibility. She married during nursing school and, over an eight-year period, had five of her own children. The day Randy (the baby) turned sixteen, Phyllis's husband died suddenly. This threw her into high gear as she became the sole provider for her children. Miraculously she managed to get the oldest ones through college.

Another tragedy would strike: Phyllis's fourth child, a boy three years older than Randy, was killed in a car accident. Phyllis was devastated, yet she persevered. Randy unfortunately, who had been plagued with infirmities since birth, didn't fare as well. He had been especially close to his deceased brother, and he grieved deeply. His mourning seemed to take a turn inward, almost as though Randy was expressing his emotional trauma through his body. His medical problems began to spin out-of-control and Phyllis, who had always found solutions, was paralyzed. Although she could always organize, get things done, accomplish, and "do," she was now facing a problem that didn't require her to "do" as much as it required her to be flexible and malleable. In short, Phyllis was having to be more adaptable than she ever had been before.

Retirement Demands Tremendous Change

Perhaps no other life change demands the breadth and depth of change that retirement does; all six arenas are directly impacted. We call upon our internal resources to undergo a sea change (a major life transformation or alteration) of activity as we rearrange our allotment of life energy among the six life arenas. Yet, what are some of the more specific changes that we are called to adopt as we make our way through retirement? Do you think healthy retirement living requests that we become:

more accepting rather than more critical?
more agreeable rather than argumentative?
more forgiving rather than judging?
more temperate rather than harsh?
more calming rather than upsetting?

These are but a few of the modifications that breed wellness and well-being in our retirement regardless of how we come to define it.

As we change we must delve deeply into ourselves and more deliberately celebrate the rhythms of our life. If we can't do this, our spiritual symphony of wholeness remains unplayed. It means our unique personal music becomes strident, simplistic, shallow, monotone, and monotonous. Retirement asks, among other things, that we bring new sections into our orchestra. It requires adaptability; we allow one section of the orchestra to fade as another section is brought into new life. Such adaptability brings a new fullness and a richer body to the symphony of our lives.

The Challenge of Personal Flexibility

Every measure of mental wellness accents the importance of flexibility, openness, malleability—adaptability. Anthropologists tell us that the primary reason that humankind has been so successful as a species on this planet is because we are the most adaptable of all living creatures. Psychologists see adaptability as the fundamental characteristic of intelligence. We demonstrate our intelligence through our adaptability. How smoothly can we fold into our daily lives the many changes that we must make throughout life? Spiritual adaptability calls us to the highest form of flexibility: accepting God's will as our own and becoming selfless in the process.

Future Shock

Many of us, without being keenly aware of it, harbor some change-inhibiting attitudes that leave us viewing change with fear and suspicion. In 1970 Alvin Toffler published his famous book titled *Future Shock*. It was an immediate bestseller and was acclaimed as a milestone work that would wield influence for years to come.

Toffler's main premise is that our culture is changing so fast that some of us simply can't keep up with it. He says that a certain segment of the population is suffering from "future shock," a condition that leaves us afraid of the future because we know it demands continuing change—and we think we have changed all that we can. He claims that "future shock" begins a cascade of physical and emotional maladies that can permanently debilitate us.

Toffler postulates that the population most at risk for "future shock" is the population of elders, because they have grown up in times when change was introduced into society at a much slower pace. As a result, that population did not learn appropriate coping, or "change skills," to manage the speed of current change. Isn't it curious that such statements as Toffler's were being made as far back as 1970. Perhaps Toffler's words are as fresh today as they were when he first outlined them.

I think Toffler was right. I call the condition "change saturation syndrome," a condition that develops when we experience great change in a short period, leaving us overloaded and overwhelmed. The pace of change is so accelerated that it doesn't give us a chance to assimilate one change before another pops up on us. As a result we begin to lose our edge, our ability to adjust and adapt to change in healthy ways.

Elders might indeed be more at risk for "change saturation syndrome," because as a group they have experienced more life history and don't want to let go of this for the sake of something unknown. Some retirees can feel assailed by change; some can even reach a point where they unconsciously say, "Enough already!" They may put their heads in the sand, so to speak, and wish the change away. We call this denial.

Change Facilitation Skills

Our worldly culture pushes us to change without break or rest. Many of us, however, think we are changing when all we're doing is running in place and not getting anywhere. We need to develop new skills that will help us move along with positive and growth-filled change. Among these "change skills" are:

1. Bringing more balance into our lives
2. Taking charge of our own morale self-management
3. Seeing new things as positive challenges, not as threats
4. Harnessing our own creativity to deal with change better
5. Developing a continuous self-improvement plan
6. Becoming more adept at taking appropriate action with the necessary responsiveness

These and several others can help us bring constructive change into our lives.

We cannot remain the same, we must change. We cannot stand still; either we move (grow) forward, or we regress (fall backward). There is no such thing as stagnation in the process we call life. We have a need for change; without change we get sick. Some retirees think that they have finally reached a time in their lives when they no longer have to change. They inadvertently push change away and seek a false life harmony by not changing, not growing. Such an attitude, although it may seem logical on the surface, is anything but growthful, anything but healthy.

Unfilled needs for change can, with time, exert tremendous

negative pressures on us. Change is a life mandate, not a luxury. Because change is something that we have always experienced, we have become dependent upon it. When change is not present we begin to regress; we open ourselves to new struggles caused by our change resistance.

I've often seen this point exhibited when I do marital counseling. In the progression of marital counseling, it's common to have one spouse point an accusing finger at the other and exclaim, "You've changed!" This emotional assault underscores the accusing partner's premise. Simply stated it would be something like: "Change isn't supposed to happen in this relationship." Clearly such an attitude is the reason that the two are in front of me for relationship counseling; one partner won't let the other adapt. One partner wants the other to remain the same person he or she was at the time of the wedding. The basic thrust of living has been blocked; naturally the marriage will suffer under this oppressive weight.

Spiritual Adaptability

Change is the watchword of the universe; the only thing that doesn't change is the fact that things are changing. Certainly God wants us to change. God doesn't want us to be the same persons we were yesterday. The change that God is looking for from us today is the same change God has been desiring for us all along: to learn how to love better. Each day, whether we're retired or not, God is saying to us: "I have given you today so that you would have the opportunity of learning how to love me better." The point is that we cannot remain the same. We are made for change, destined for adaptability. We find it in positive ways such as personal growth and development, or we resist it through anger, depression, anxiety, or generalized angst. On a religious level, the ultimate change is conversion and redemption. Yet whether we resist change or embrace it, we will deal with it.

Adaptability vs. Rigidity

The premier power needed to pull us through this tenth retirement success factor is adaptability. Adaptability includes adjusting to surrounding conditions and surviving as an agreeable person. Spiritual adaptability is taking on the ways of God, adopting God's will by harmonizing ourselves with heaven. The opposite characteristic is rigidity.

Rigidity blocks us from growing, stops us from addressing the life changes that we must. Rigidity offers the illusion that we can remain as we are; it robs us of moving closer to our true Selves and closer to God.

Affirmation

Dear Lord, help me become all that I can be in my retirement. I know that retirement brings more change than perhaps any other age or stage of life. I also know that these changes will challenge me fully. Throughout all this I need your help, dear Lord, in remaining as flexible and as adaptable as I can be. I know that adaptability comes from You, dear Lord, and so I might even refer to it as "holy adaptability." Help me to see where I might be unknowingly blocking changes that I may need to fold into my lifestyle. Let me fully realize that retirement is a time for accelerated growth, it is not a time where I simply "mark time" and rest on the accomplishments of the past. I know that You placed me here on this earth so that I would change, so that I would learn better how to love, and therefore grow closer to You, dear Lord.

CHAPTER 11

Live "Now"

*What is the only absolutely certain human condition that will
exist from the moment of birth throughout
an entire lifetime to the moment of death?
Change.*

SHAD HELMSTETTER

Retirement Success Pearl #11

Spiritual Luster: The degree that you can live in the
"now" and experience the glow of the light of Christ,
understand your inner beauty, and recognize your spiritual distinctiveness.

Retirement Challenge #11: How can I remain as fully
alive in retirement as I did in previous life stages?

Developing the Art of Living NOW: Rich's Story

Rich has been retired for more than four years. He and his wife decided that they would remain where they live, because two of their three children live nearby and being near the kids was something they both wanted.

While not a man to claim any special holiness, Rich clearly enjoyed his faith. He liked going to services, liked the people he had known for many years, and liked the notion of being associated with a church. It gave him a home, a place where he belonged, and a site of worship. He loved all this.

Rich liked people in general and so it seemed natural that he would find ways of socializing. What evolved, however, was nothing that he could have ever guessed. Slowly but steadily, Rich began showing up each morning at the local McDonald's restaurant. He didn't know how it started, but the group had grown to over fifteen guys who met every morning just to "chew the fat," starting about 7:00 A.M. The restaurant offers a seniors discount and all the coffee you can drink. Some guys stay for as long as two hours; Rich usually spends about an hour. He likes seeing the guys, some from the church, others from his former work place, and some simply from the neighborhood.

Although he liked having a place to go each morning where he could talk with the other guys, Rich began to notice that the topics for discussion all seemed to center around the past. Many of the guys repeated stories from their work, vacations of years ago, military experiences, sports memories, and metro-area histories. While the stories were interesting, they were all from the past. Certainly reminiscing is a positive and growthful thing to pursue, and Rich enjoyed that aspect of the conversations. But he didn't like the theme that he thought he heard running through the stories.

At first this theme was subtle and Rich thought he might just be too sensitive about the issue. Eventually, however, he could clearly hear the undercurrent of judgment and criticism in every story: the way things were "back then" is the way they are supposed to be. There emerged an apparent prejudice that "yesterday" was better. The stories seemed to end in the assumption that "ain't it awful how things are today." It struck Rich that this group of men, as good as they were, seemed to have lost their luster.

Rich didn't know what to do. He tried to change the subject several times but didn't get very far. He tried to give the stories a current focus, but that too seemed anemic under the press to paint the past as glorious and the present as second-rate.

Pretty soon, Rich found himself skipping a day here and there: a "day off." Gradually, his "days off" became more numerous, and now he goes only one or two days a week. He feels awkward about this because he believes he's the only one who doesn't lament the passing of the "good ol' days of yesterday." He doesn't know for sure, however, since he never brought it up to the group.

Retirement and the NOW

The degree to which we "live in the past," or believe that we were "better" in the past, will create psychological barriers preventing full development and growth in retirement. There is an all too common tendency in some retirees to regard a past point in time as their pinnacle of performance, and hence the time when "I was at my best." Although both men and women experience this, women seem to encounter it earlier in life then men and have, therefore, generally crossed the bridge into acceptance of lost power, ability, or beauty earlier than men. Men may be facing this transition into acceptance for the first time at the retirement decision point. Some never face it at all.

There is a cultural tendency to overvalue "young" and undervalue "old." Doesn't this seem somewhat illogical at face value? Why would we value a state of life that is inexperienced and unknowing more than a state that is experienced and knowledgeable? This tendency to inflate the value of youth has a corresponding effect of deflating maturation. We perceive those human developmental tasks of our younger years as "good," and those of our later years as "bad." Such notions naturally prejudice our later years as decremental. Yet, why would we think that learning to walk at sixteen months of age is a more growth-filled than learning to use the body at a slower pace at age seventy-five? Personal growth and development means mastering life lessons at every stage of our life span.

If we ask ourselves, "Would I rather be eighty or twenty? seventy or thirty? sixty or forty?" we might respond, "I want to be the age I am right now." However, when we ask ourselves, "When was I the most successful, effective, efficient?" most of us would point to yesterday's successes. "When was I most challenged?" Again, "Yesterday, before I went 'over the hill.'"

Attitudes like these, which we encounter every day, devalue our innate growth imperative. The fact is that every age of our lives is good, bursting with developmental potential. Yet we erroneously think that as we grow "over the hill," whenever and wherever that hill may be, our past personal triumphs, our achievements of yesterday, our successes of earlier times, were more impressive, gutsy, and "real" compared to anything we accomplish today, as we journey "beyond the hill."

Now is the only time we can live, and *now* is the only time we can love! Yesterday offers no opportunity for heeding God's call to love today. God is only now; God's name is not "I was" or "I will be." God is the great "I Am." Unless we respond to God's call of love today, we diminish our potential for living fully. When we choose to live in yesterday, we choose love's shadow. We devalue ourselves by settling for mediocrity; we make excuses for being less than who we really are; we let our internal light begin to fade; we lose our vitality, verve, and vibrancy.

Such subtle ageism gnaws at our being and reinforces our belief in this process called aging. Perhaps the most insidious aspect of this attitude is that we run the risk of giving ourselves permission to become less demanding of ourselves, less apt to put forth concentrated effort, less desirous of achievement. We go and get the excuse, "I'm 'over the hill.' I'm getting old, and old means less...."—whatever we need an excuse for. With such self-talk we risk becoming intellectually stale and losing our emotional freshness, attitudinal vitality, cognitive edge, sense of loving and living. In a word, we lose our luster.

Spiritual Luster

Did you ever wonder why some people seem to sparkle, have a gleam in their eyes, and the hint of a smile on their face all the time? You know who they are when you're with them, and so does everyone else. This is the quality we call spiritual luster. Luster is a personal, intangible quality that speaks of inner radiance, glow, and personal brilliance. Luster is that complex characteristic that allows each of us to remain alive, vital, and zest-filled. Luster is the opposite of growing stale; it is that attractive spark of motivation that allows people full expression of themselves in the present. Luster serves as an uplifting preventative buffer against thinking that things were better "back when." "I was better when I was younger. Isn't it too bad that I've lost all those years." Luster is present focused, positive, and loving—inwardly and outwardly.

There are three qualities of luster that are particularly attractive for people of faith. First, luster has luminosity, an inner radiance or brilliance that comes from the inside. We are people of light and we are called to let our light shine. We don't put our light under a basket; rather, we put it on a pedestal and let the world see it. This is not being boastful. Rather, it's knowing that we were created quite intentionally by God and that the light we can reflect into the dark world is unlike anyone else's light. If we don't reflect our light, then that particular, unique light that

God has given to us alone will not shine at all; and we will have no luster. No one else can shine our light. We are called, each and every day, to become luminous to the degree that our own specialness comes out. We don't produce this light, of course; only God produces light. But we are called to reflect God's light as only we can.

The second characteristic of spiritual luster is beauty. We are innately attractive at our core. Regardless of how we think we look on our exterior, we are beautiful on the inside. It is this beauty that makes us the individuals we are. This attractiveness is our real selves, and it is this attractiveness that we must come to own. We must come to possess our own beauty, to believe in it, to know it.

The third characteristic of spiritual luster is distinctiveness. No one else is made like we are as individuals. God did, indeed, throw away the mold when each of us emerged into our physical, emotional, psychological, and spiritual uniqueness. We *are* unique, one of a kind, like no other. We are called to be that unique person. Our luster shines when we are ourselves, not when we try to copy someone else, not when we judge ourselves to be less than what we actually are.

I believe that if we could really see our luster—really penetrate to our very core and experience our unique light, our true beauty and special distinctiveness—we would be nearly blinded by the magnificence of it all. Perhaps it is a good thing that we can't see it all at once, because if we could we might never return to this earth. We are that wonderful! Luster gives us self-affirmation, balance, humor, and personal motivation. When we lose our luster; we lose our ability to relax, be committed, resilient, and real. We become lackluster!

The point of this retirement success factor of life span spiritual development is that all this light, beauty, and distinctiveness is there in us at every stage of life. We didn't somehow expend our spiritual luster somewhere back in our past. We are called to tap into our luster and open any blocked portals of light that may be plugged with erroneous beliefs about ourselves at the age and condition we experience right now.

Now is the time to show our luster. Now is the time to be who we truly are and were truly meant to be. God expects nothing else, because anything less than this means we are in some state of separation from God, a condition that is sometimes called sin, and a condition that points to our own brokenness.

Ten Components of Spiritual Luster

While spiritual luster has these three overarching concepts that hold it together, when we ask other people of faith what particular personality characteristics create the life condition of spiritual luster we find that the following ten components rate the highest:

1. Prayerful: person of faith, reflective, contemplative
2. Faith driven: connected to God, virtuous, motivated by love, envisions and practices peace and justice
3. Real: genuine, authentic, bone fide, good self-esteem
4. Radiator of Christ's peace: in harmony, lives life as gift, reflects beauty
5. Committed: steadfast, stamina, staying power, confident
6. Balanced: whole, integrated, developmentally on track
7. Affirming of self: encouraging, a positive force, constructive, empowering
8. A good listener: gives full attention, perceptive, aware
9. Respectful: considerate, attentive, allows others to be who they are, altruistic
10. Optimistic: hopeful, positive thinking, able to influence good.

Wisdom vs. Inadequacy

Wisdom is the grace-filled power that propels us through this retirement success factor of life span spiritual development. Wisdom is the prudent, sane, and sensible use of accumulated knowledge. Wisdom includes the ability to discern inner qualities, have insight, practice good sense and sound judgment. Spiritually, wisdom includes recognizing God's presence in others, having singularity of purpose, and being spiritually insightful—seeing what is not at first concretely apparent. The opposite of wisdom is inadequacy.

Inadequacy refers to the illusions of personal insufficiency that sometimes overtake us. Inadequacy renders our thinking: shallow, clouded, ill-conceived, and absurd. Inadequacy contorts our efforts by preventing us from changing in ways that make us better.

Affirmation

My identity is in today, not in yesterday, nor in tomorrow. Help me dear Lord to treasure what is right in front of me. Help me to cherish the moment, notice the beauty right here, right now, appreciate the aroma of life today, and always give thanks. Let me focus my attention not upon the things of this world, rather let me focus from the center of my heart onto the true meaning of my life. Let me fully recognize that yesterday is an empty container; it can never be captured again. So, dear Lord, let me raise my gaze from yesterday to today, and not be troubled about tomorrow. Truly, today is the only day that I can live, it is the only day that I can love; help me remember always that I am called to both today. I cannot live and love yesterday, and I cannot live and love tomorrow. It is only in today where I can find you, dear Lord. Help me in my quest to know my genuine luster, dear Lord: to fully see your light inside of me, to understand my inner beauty, and to recognize my true spiritual distinctiveness.

CHAPTER 12

Honor Yourself

You cannot honor another person by dishonoring yourself.

R. P. Johnson

Retirement Success Pearl #12

Caregiving Responsibility: The degree that you can honor yourself and become free from a sense of burden or strain from caregiving responsibilities for aging parents, relatives, adult children, and/or friends.

Retirement Challenge #12: How can I honor my aging parents, relatives, adult children, and/or friends without dishonoring myself?

Eleanor's Story: The Conflicts of Caregiving

Eleanor was crossing the big river bridge when she remembered that she had not called her mother before leaving on her weekend trip to visit her friend. She knew what that would mean: Mother would be upset and hurt. Eleanor had tried everything to tell her mother that she does, indeed, love her very much, and certainly wants the best for her. Yet, over the past year her mother's needs seemed to escalate to the point where Eleanor was starting to show signs of weariness. At times, she probably appeared to be short tempered with her mother. Why was her mother needing more and more of Eleanor's attentions and affections?

Eleanor is a widow; her husband died in an automobile accident ten years ago. Her three children are all on their own, leaving Eleanor with the family house. After her husband died, Eleanor managed to steady herself emotionally and invested lots of energy in her job. She had worked since her children were in high school, but after her husband's death, her career began to soar. She was promoted to office manager, and then regional manager of a toy distributorship. She enjoyed her work and found that it offered her a new sense of personal fulfillment that she had never experienced. Yet, Eleanor was feeling more and more pulled by her own desires to do things she couldn't while working full time.

The friend Eleanor was visiting was retired and encouraged her to "hang it up" and go have some fun in her life. Eleanor longed to do just that—to relax, travel, and have time for herself, to do the things she always wanted to do. Yet, every time she began thinking seriously about retiring she was stopped in her tracks by her mother's needs. She knew that her work provided a safe haven for her, insulating her from spending more time with her mother. She reasoned that if she didn't work, her mother would expect that much more of her. She also knew that she would be so affected by guilt that she probably couldn't say "no" to her mother's requests. If she retired, Eleanor was sure that she would end up over at her mother's house every day and, eventually, her mother would want to move in with her, or visa versa.

Eleanor loved her mother and wanted to go on loving her. But she innately knew that she could get caught in her mother's sometimes desperate neediness, which Eleanor truly believed was more emotionally based than arising from physical circumstances. Eleanor knew her mother was somewhat dependent and that being around more would not help her mother. In fact, Eleanor reasoned, her mother would probably get worse. She would become more dependent and adopt more of a "patient" role rather than growing into a gracious elder woman. This dependency was something that Eleanor could hardly take. She had experienced it in her mother for years; it was Eleanor who always had to pick up the pieces from her mother's fragmented life.

Eleanor wanted to retire, and she was certainly ready, but retirement would not mean a new freedom for her. Rather, it would probably mean a new confinement, one that would be much harder to tolerate than the confinement her work created. Consequently, Eleanor felt like she could not retire; she had to "stay the course" of working, not because she needed work, but because it prevented her from becoming caught in her mother's dependent personality.

Putting Off the Retirement Transition

The research is clear: those of us who have caregiving responsibilities generally tend to continue in the lifestyle we have carved out; we tend not to change. This may prevent some of us from freely entering into retirement. Yet, each of us is called to enter into the compassionate caregiving that Christ modeled for us. The question is, how far can we go? Are there boundaries to our caregiving? How do we prevent dishonoring ourselves? How can we live out Christ's commandment to love deeply and serve others, especially our parents and other elders, without losing pieces of ourselves along the way?

Christ commanded us to love one another. The meaning of the fourth commandment, the so-called "caregivers commandment" is certainly clear. Yet, how much of ourselves are we supposed to give? Like Eleanor, we tend to put off our retirement decision when we know that others are dependent on us. It doesn't matter if the dependent person is an elder parent or an adult child, the fact that others are dependent on us is the crucial issue that puts up a barrier blocking a smooth retirement transition.

The question, however, is not "do" we care for another, but "how" can we go about this business of caregiving. In my counseling practice I encounter many wonderful people of faith who become emotional contorted and psychologically pained due to internal conflicts they feel over caring for others. More often than not, they are in turmoil over caring for their aging parents; although adult children, spouses, and relatives can also escalate the burden of care well beyond their comfort and tolerance levels.

Each of us varies dramatically in the amount of "felt responsibility" we experience for others. Some of us feel deeply about the welfare of others, while some of us seem rather disinterested or deny the needs of others. When it comes to retirement, our felt responsibility for others can impact us greatly, positively or negatively. What would otherwise be a smooth transition into our retirement lifestyle may become stormy indeed when the strain of caring for elders (or other family members) becomes overwhelming.

It is not uncommon for elder caregivers to feel a barrage of negative feelings regarding their caregiving endeavors: fear, anger, sadness, and guilt to name only a few. Indeed, we can sometimes see a new sibling rivalry emerge: contention over how best to deal with Mom or Dad now that they are older. Even marital discord can rear its head when one marriage partner is pressed into caregiving service of a parent, especially when this service becomes chronic. Vitality can drain from a marriage when one partner is overinvolved with a parent. Finally, and probably most importantly, for the caregiver is the fact that caregiving can erode our health. Research has shown that caregiving can elevate stress levels enough to trigger various physical and emotional maladies.

The Expanding Need for Caregiving

The need for care is expanding in our culture. The medical community seems ever more creative in devising ways to keep our bodies alive. While we are grateful, this creates tremendous caregiving responsibilities for families. Families have been there in the past, they are there today, and they must continue to be there in the future to care for their elder members. Yet today's modern families, including retirees, may not be fully equipped for the task that confronts them. Without the help they need, well-intentioned caregivers, many of whom may be nearing retirement or are already retired, are at risk of giving away their last ounce of stamina in the service of helping others. We cannot honor God's children by dishonoring ourselves.

How can this caregiving endeavor become energy enhancing rather than energy sapping? Is there a way for caregiving to become spiritually uplifting rather than draining?

Retirees—and all caregivers, for that matter—require six ingredients that inject caregiving with spiritual dynamism rather than emotional pain. Caregivers need to

1. Gain understanding into the needs of their elders as well as their own
2. Develop truly healthy relationships with their aging parents
3. Know how to break down barriers that may exist between themselves and their aging parents

4. Foster positive communication between themselves and their aging parents
5. Allow Christ's healing message to become the core of their relationship
6. Remember that death and mourning are the final end of the caregiving process when dealing with aging parents.

When properly incorporated into the caregiving situation, these six ingredients have the power to transform a potential travail of uncertainty and frustration into a time of spiritual development unparalleled in one's previous life stages. There is no other place where the virtues of hope, mercy, acceptance, strength, perseverance, kindness, and simplicity can be better learned than in the caregiving situation. God offers us the challenges of caregiving as a part of our curriculum for spiritual growth. While we know the outcome of our caregiving efforts—someday our caregiving will end when our parent dies—it's in the process of caregiving that we gain the soulful stamina and spiritual fortitude that can propel us to holy ground and celestial heights. The power of the experience of caregiving is beyond the material plane; it resides solidly on God's plateau of holiness. It is on this glorious plateau that we find the treasure of caregiving that is our inheritance.

Retirement is a gift, actually many gifts in each of the arenas of our lives. God calls us to first recognize our giftedness, be grateful for the gifts, and finally to share the many gifts we have been given. It is in so doing that we come to truly see the truth, beauty, and goodness of our special status as children of God in our retirement lifestyle.

Steadfastness vs. Unreliable

The motive power for energizing this retirement success factor is steadfastness. Steadfastness is remaining fixed in place, immovable, unfaltering, and being confident and sure of movement, unfaltering. On a spiritual plane, steadfastness is being firm in belief, staunch, resolute, and loyal. The opposite is being unreliable.

The opposite of steadfastness is being unreliable. Unreliability means being irresponsible, untrustworthy, and unsure. It renders a person undependable, prone to breaking down, and easily pushed "off-track."

(For more information on the caregiving role and practical suggestions on how to honor your aging parent, see Dr. Johnson's book titled *How to Honor Your Aging Parents: Fundamental Principles of Caregiving.* Liguori Lifespan, 1999.)

Affirmation

Lord, help me shoulder whatever caregiving responsibilities that are mine in ways that build me rather than tear me down. I want to follow your lead, Lord, and reflect your love to those that I love, too. Yet sometimes I find that I can overextend myself. With only the best of intentions, I begin to lose parts of me and feel fragmented and in turmoil. Lord, help me to catch myself before some of my perceptions, thoughts, and feelings begin to set beyond the horizon of healthy motivation and cause me to lose sight of your light, leaving me in personal strain and at risk for sickness of some kind. Help me become more awake to this process of disconnecting from You which I can fall into quite unintentionally. When I do fall, when I do unknowingly disconnect from You, I feel so sad, so angry, so guilty, and so wounded. Oh, Lord, grant me the power of steadfastness so I can rise to the level of caring, the level of honoring that is most helpful, most growthful for all, and certainly most connected to You.

CHAPTER 13

"Get Connected"

There is something self-renewing in love.

Thomas Moore

Retirement Success Pearl #13

Home Life: The degree to which you can become connected with and derive satisfaction, intimacy, love, and a sense of well-being from your primary (marital) relationship and/or your family life.

Retirement Challenge #13: How can I find a sustaining sense of connectedness in my retirement years with those closest to me?

Your Need for Being Connected: William's Dilemma

William breathed a sigh of relief as he closed the kitchen door behind him and headed for the garage on his morning ritual of leaving for work, which had started an hour earlier at 5:30 A.M. He loved his wife, Debra, but he had recognized some time ago that too much of a good thing was simply too much. He actually looked forward to work; it provided him an escape, a safety valve, that relieved the pressure caused by too much contact with Debra.

Today he felt particularly perplexed because the final date for accepting the special "early-out" retirement package was only a week away—and he hadn't yet told Debra about it. The company was offering a severance package for his over twenty-five years of service. If he took the package, he could retire now, more than five years earlier than he had anticipated. But why hadn't he told Debra? What was he hiding from?

He knew why: he found himself relating less and less positively with Debra. He wanted to be kind and thoughtful, compassionate and considerate. Yet every time he tried, some string would be pulled at a deep place within him, and his positive feelings would collapse in on themselves. What would come out was lukewarm at best. So often his communication with Debra became toxic. He wasn't telling Debra about the early-out package because he knew that Debra would urge him to take it. If he refused to accept it, she would immediately know that he was stalling. She would assume that her husband was choosing work over spending time with her.

William didn't blame Debra, nor did he blame himself for the marital impasse that had infected their marriage. He knew that they needed to work it out together. Yet it was the togetherness that was the problem. They really hadn't learned to communicate positively with each other; rather, they sniped and snapped. They respected and loved each other, but their communication pattern was anything but loving. In fact, William always felt like he had to explain his very presence to Debra; it seemed that just walking into a room would cause her to throw out some caustic remark. Naturally, he would oblige her remark with one of his own. He knew that he was fostering the miscommunications as much as Debra was, yet he simply didn't know what to do.

William never did tell Debra about the early-out opportunity; the deadline came and went without William making a move. In not making a move, William chose to continue working; he chose to continue the tired status quo of emotional distance to which his marriage had descended.

The Common Story

William's story is not uncommon. Countless marriages simply limp along in their confused pain, ragged interactions, and communication ruts. The challenge of retirement success factor thirteen is: How can we find a sustaining sense of connectedness with those closest to us in our retirement years? A marriage like William and Debra's creates a mammoth block preventing them from enjoying the joy of the relationships that God intended. It lacks one or more of the six essential components of a truly healthy marriage: (1) mutuality, (2) respect, (3) positive communication, (4) intimacy, (5) trust, and (6) staying power.

1. *Mutuality:* The human relationship condition created when each partner thoroughly believes she or he is a principal in a union of common purpose, and where each partner's overall needs are valued equally, creating an egalitarian union of interdependence and a shared conviction of togetherness.
2. *Respect:* The human relationship condition created when each partner sees the uniqueness of the other. Each partner's personal specialness is honored and cherished by the other partner as a part of the gift of the marriage.

3. *Positive communication:* The human relationship
   thinking condition created when each partner uses the
   language of caring and compassion, spends quality time
   together with their partner, and can work out the inevitable differences that emerge in all relationships by using
   quality interaction skills.
4. *Intimacy:* The human relationship feeling condition created by a strong and positive emotional bond, an almost
   mystical bond, that produces devotion, attachment,
   and affection between relationship partners, and which
   sometimes requires personal sacrifice.
5. *Trust:* The human relationship deciding condition created
   when each partner can rely upon the other without question, when each partner exercises progressive competencies
   in negotiating change, and when each partner willingly
   anticipates, expects, and facilitates their partner's growth
   and development as a human being of dynamic worth.
6. *Staying power:* The human relationship action condition
   created when each partner exercises personal perseverance, patience, and steadfastness so fidelity and coura-
   geous commitment can grow strong over a lifetime.

If we were to rate William's vision of his marriage using these
six marriage conditions as our yardstick, how would the marriage fare? On a scale of one to ten, with ten indicating that these
marriage conditions exist to a high degree in their marriage, and
one indicating that they exist to a low degree, William's view of
his marriage might look something like this:

1. *Mutuality: 7.* The marriage does seem to focus on the two
   of them. There is an "us" in the marriage. Even though the
   interaction pattern is disturbed, William senses that the
   partners do know that they are "center stage" for each other.
   There does seem to be a "togetherness" in this marriage.

2. *Respect: 6.* While there seems to be little respect on the surface of the marriage, that is, in the day-to-day operation of the marriage, William still seems to maintain a substantial degree of respect for Debra at deeper levels. Unfortunately, both partners display this respect all too infrequently, though underneath they do seem to have the basis for a positive consideration for each other.

3. *Positive communication: 3.* From William's description, the marriage seems to suffer under the duress of fragmented and caustic communications. William portrays a picture of a marriage in which the two partners rarely focus on each other's feelings; they seem wounded by aspects of their own feelings and seek to communicate this hurt to their partner by sniping at each other. This behavior sets up an endless cycle of hurt and counter-hurt, ending in emotional distance and "stuffed" feelings.

4. *Intimacy: 4.* Intimacy means sharing one's inner core, those parts that are most tender and meaningful. This marriage unfortunately does not perform this task. Given William's evaluation of the marriage, it seems that the partners are frightened that they will be discounted, criticized. or ridiculed, or that the information will be used against each other at some later time. All this constrains the free flow of affection and thwarts intimacy on all levels.

5. *Trust: 6.* William seems to trust Debra. He has acknowledged that Debra will "be there" for him. Yet this trust only regards the functional parts of the relationship: income, meal preparation, smooth running of the home, family obligations. The trust does not extend to the psychological or spiritual parts of the individual. When this level of trust is absent, any marriage languishes. It lacks energy, life, and sparkle.

6. *Staying power: 9.* For William, this is the strongest com-

ponent of his marriage to Debra. They have been together for a long time, and neither of them has any intention of leaving the life security of the relationship. They will limp along, however, experiencing only half a marriage for the duration.

Since our story of William and Debra is generally told from William's viewpoint, we don't have an accurate picture of how Debra might rate these same six relationship conditions. Debra may see the relationships from an entirely different vantage point, and therefore give entirely different ratings here. The point is that each of us sees our relationships quite differently.

These six components of a close relationship can be applied to a significant personal relationship as well as to marriage. We use the term "confidante" to describe the roles persons play for each other when each can feel free to share their very soul. Having a confidante offers us perhaps the most potent vehicle for well being that we will ever have. If you have a confidante, take very good care of that person; if you don't have a confidante—get one!

Christ's Message of Relatedness

Christ's message to us is a message of relatedness. In order for us to love one another, we must truly connect with others. It is there, in that connection, where we find our true selves; we find ourselves reflected in others. Research into interpersonal relatedness has determined that persons who have developed capacities and competencies for sharing themselves with others are among the most emotionally healthy people. Sharing our unique selves seems marvelously growth-filled; it allows our inner potential to take root and come to flower.

What is it that we are supposed to share with others? Simply stated, we are called to share ourselves. First, we share our time, talents, and possessions. Second, on a deeper level, we share our inner lives: our joys, fears, hopes, dreams, desires, mistakes, and faith. All this and more is the "stuff" of our lives, and the personal material we are privileged to use as connectors with others. This profound sharing on a personal level is called "intimacy." Those who can create and sustain relationships characterized by intimacy generally are the most healthy among us.

We are lucky, indeed, to be able to relate, connect, or find intimacy with a wide range of persons. For example, we share some of our "self" with waitresses, bank tellers, store clerks. Naturally we do not share deeply but, nonetheless, we share a segment of our wants, needs, and desires. Perhaps we share a bit more deeply with our neighbors, coworkers, and acquaintances. Deeper still, we find our friends, pals, buddies, perhaps our golf partners. With these folks we may find that we share even more. Then comes our good friends, personal friends, and best friends. Finally, there are those persons with whom we share most fully: our confessor, spouse, confidante. Here is the range of our intimacy; the breadth of our personal sharing. The more and better we can continue this sharing in retirement, the more satisfied we will ultimately be with life. Retirement challenges us to share at even deeper levels than we did before.

In his deeply thoughtful book, *Redemptive Intimacy: A New Perspective for the Journey to Adult Faith*, Dick Westley tells us that "the Lord dwells not in images, laws, or rituals, not in Jerusalem, Mecca, or even Rome, but in people, in our noblest parts where justice and charity dwell." Personal experience for Westley is revelatory; and "gathering to share and get in touch with that experience" is a "dialogue of faith sharing in the name of the Lord" (page 8).

Intimacy seems fundamental to our faith development. It is in sharing deeply with others that we find Jesus reflected, as we look into the interior and find the love that motivates all. Through our active listening and presence to other persons of faith, we find our true self. We find God incarnate in our intimacy with others; here in this community of faith we are better able to enter more fully into the adventure of recognizing God in every part of our lives.

The opposite of connectedness is reclusiveness. Unfortunately, reclusiveness is no stranger to many retirees. Aloneness breeds loneliness when there's no one around with whom to connect, or when we build our own shells of protection, insulating ourselves from others—and from ourselves. Reclusiveness constricts our souls, strangles our life energy, and cuts us away from the vitality of living. We become sour, dour, self-absorbed, and cantankerous. Without intimacy we risk becoming alienated. Alienation bores into our hearts in three ways. First, it slowly erodes whatever lines of connection we formerly enjoyed with others. Second, it shears us away from our essential self. Third, it separates us from God.

More retirements are ruined by this factor than by perhaps any other. All other success factors can be tightly "in place," yet if this one is broken, all the others seem hollow by comparison. There are many good counselors who can work with relationships. They can help partners overcome some of the hang-ups that encumber their relationship, allowing them to find a new, rich, intimate communion.

Love vs. Fear

Love is the power that opens the way for deeper relationships, even to the point of intimacy and communion. Love is almost indefinable, yet the concepts of holding one dear, pursuing holiness, blessedness, and wholeness bring us closer to understanding it. The opposite of love is fear.

Fear stifles us by paralyzing our relationships infecting them with doubt and suspicion, jealousy and envy. All this leads to guilt and anger. Eventually fear brings us to the precipice of revenge seeking rather than seeking complementarity.

Affirmation

Lord, You know what makes for a humanly healthy relationship; You also know what makes for a spiritually healthy relationship. Lord, help me to gradually learn how to inject these fundamental principles into my primary relationship. I so wish that my relationship can grow into all that it's supposed to become. Help me to value my loved ones, to respect their wishes and needs, to communicate clearly and lovingly, to create strong emotional bonds with them, to willingly trust them, and to persevere with them through difficult times. Help me find deep intimacy in those close to me and especially in that one person who is closest. Help me see in that person reflections of You as I gaze deeply into this most cherished person.

CHAPTER 14

Become Ageless

Aging is not a thief in the night.
Aging is our master teacher.
R. P. JOHNSON

Retirement Success Pearl #14

Maturation Vitality: The degree to which you see your maturation process (aging) as a time of emotional and spiritual vitality and vibrancy full of potential for dynamic and ongoing personal growth.

Retirement Challenge #14: How do I grow in youthfulness as I advance in maturity?

How to Become Ageless: Terry's Trial

Terry looked around at the other drivers waiting with him for the light to turn green. He wondered where they were all going, what were they doing. He was only making a trip to the drug store to pick up yet another prescription for his arthritis. "This isn't a trip I want to make," he mused, "It's something I'm forced to do."

Shortly after he retired two years ago Terry started feeling his age. It seemed like everywhere he went—the drug store, the bank, restaurants, department stores, video stores, church—he found himself mentally assessing the age of other people, and comparing himself to them. It seemed that he was always the oldest.

Terry struggled with this frame of oldness that he was putting around himself. Each time he did this mental calculation, as he did at the stoplight, he felt further and further removed from the mainstream of life. He seemed to be pushing himself away from considering himself a true part of society. He was no longer working and now, on top of that, he saw himself as old. The combination scared, angered him, saddened him.

As his retirement continued, Terry found himself becoming more irritable, more removed from opportunities for social interaction, and more inclined to stay home and watch TV; generally, Terry was becoming a "couch potato." He found himself focusing more and more on his body. Doctor appointments became more frequent, giving his life its main definition. He measured his calendar not by days, weeks, and months like he used to, but by his doctor visits' his whole life seemed to revolve around.

One day, his primary-care physician asked Terry a ridiculous question—at least that's what Terry thought. "Terry," he asked, "do you think that you're depressed?"

At first Terry was offended by the question. He had always been known as a high energy, resourceful, strong, and self-possessed individual. How could his doctor ask this question? What gave him the impression that Terry might be depressed?

Although Terry defensively denied that he was depressed, he gave the question more serious consideration later that night. He read the small flyer on depression that his doctor had given him and, incredulously, he found himself fitting almost every one of the specific criteria for depression. "How did I come to this?" he questioned. "Am I in that bad of shape?"

Terry eventually took hold of himself. He returned to his doctor, was placed on antidepressant medication, and began seeing a counselor. He learned that he had always harbored a decidedly pessimistic attitude about aging. Because both his parents had died early, Terry hadn't had contact with older persons who showed examples of vitality and personal growth, examples that may have changed his mind about aging. Terry had merely accepted the negative stereotypes about aging that pervade our media. Without ever clarifying his attitudes, Terry believed that aging had little, if anything, positive to offer. Now this attitude had surfaced with a destructiveness that tore at the heart of his retirement and stopped him from entering a life of freedom and heightened personal development. In short, Terry didn't have a clue of what positive and creative aging was all about. He certainly didn't look at aging as a special time that God had given him so that he could learn more clearly who he was at his core.

Aging and Retirement

Our view of aging—our internal perception of what the aging process means to us at the very depths of our being—can mean the difference between a retirement filled with growth and personal expression, and one devoid of life, filled with timidity, tremor, tiredness, even terror. The choice is ours, because it is in our own attitudes that we wage this battle between a regressive and progressive view of retirement and later-life living. When we develop an enlightened view of aging we are free to invest ourselves fully into the love lessons that later-life living brings.

The degree to which we do not embrace our own maturation process, and come to a fuller appreciation of its value, is the degree to which we will fight retirement and ultimately fight ourselves. Such a fight leads to personal depletion, uncertainty, bitterness, sorrow, hurt, and confusion.

It's regrettable that retirement is so connected to aging. It really doesn't have to be so at all. Certainly retirement normally arrives at the later portion of a person's life, yet through the miracles of modern science and a robust economy, our retirement phase of living can last longer than any other life stage. This is a profound revelation. Yet, many of us still hobble around with an outmoded perception of retirement as being that which you do when you don't have the energy to do anything else.

Thankfully, this definition is dying, and a new definition of retirement is emerging that reveals a time of life filled with vibrancy, verve, and vitality. This idea can be recognized on both the physical plane and the spiritual plane. This new growthful notion of retirement and later-life living needs to be unfurled and waved for all to see.

Need We Become Old?

As we continue to advance in maturity, need we become old? We seem to ascribe certain behaviors, feelings, attitudes, and perceptions to those of us who are "old." Without our conscious awareness, we often project these illusionary ideas about aging onto ourselves and those around us. Confusing matters even more, we perceive the developmental tasks of our younger years as "good," while the tasks of our later years seem to be unfortunate, even unnecessary.

Why do some persons only forty-five years old seem ancient, while other persons, even well beyond ninety, reflect a lightness and brightness we associate with behavior much, much earlier in the life span? How old, or youthful, do you feel? What forces contribute to the ongoing preservation and, indeed, the development of youthfulness across the life span?

Youthfulness

Youthfulness is that creative quality in the God-conscious realm of our mind—the spiritual level—that sustains and intensifies our involvement in life in ways that enable us to thrive regardless of our chronological age. Youthfulness is blind to age. One could even say that being young hinders the development of youthfulness; one must be very mature to exhibit youthfulness. Youthfulness is an attitude of vitality, freshness, and honesty that brings color, life, and love to a person.

What are these behavioral outcomes of the quality of youthfulness? To become youthful in its full spiritual sense, we must consciously

1. *Transform our attitudes about aging:* We've been aging all our life. Aging is one of God's principle means for transforming our lives, for initiating our personal conversion. Aging calls us to view ourselves in the light of God as never before. In retirement, we are called to change our image of aging from that of a "thief in the night," who strips us of all that is dear to us, to an image of the "master teacher," who can mentor our spiritual learning. Aging is a reminder of our new life in the Spirit. Such a view transcends the negativism that our culture ascribes to aging. We come to see aging not as an end, but as another beginning of our journey to God.

2. *Resolve old conflicts:* Grudges are a poison to the soul and a toxin to the body. The internal bitterness of old grudges debilitates and enfeebles the most robust among us, making us lonely old men and women who moan out in disgust at the personal robbery that we think is taking place within us.

3. *Offer something of ourselves to others:* Altruism—giving

freely of our ourselves to others—produces wellness. Giving calms the body and invigorates the spirit, makes us part of the motion and energy of the universe, and merges us with the primary motive force of heaven, because it is a reflection of God. If we are serious about our own wellness, we will be serious about finding ways to help others—daily. Service, stewardship, and servanthood build us up, making us healthy, happy, and in harmony with our fellow human beings, our world, and our God.

4. *Develop a grateful heart:* What decision are we making right now about our life: miser or master? Misers grab and squeezes the life out of everything they touch, while masters affirm the truth, beauty, and goodness of what is presented to them. Are we misers or masters?

5. *Can laugh at ourselves:* Humor salves the emotional chaffing that can be a part of aging. It thumbs its nose at the changes aging brings by demonstrating the essential absurdity of the possibility that we could be anything but loveable children of God. Humor transcends the gravity and edges out the fear that the world embraces as its reaction to aging. Humor makes us light, bright, and ready to embrace life with renewed zest and vigor.

6. *Continues to expand oneself:* Learning new things stimulates the mind, invigorates the body, and unfetters the spirit. It injects sparkle, pep, and exhilaration into an otherwise mundane landscape. Finding new ways to stretch ourselves allows us to remain part of the unfolding of this plane, and thereby part of the human drama always emerging here. Cultivating a sustaining interest in things outside ourselves gives us youthfulness.

7. *Engages in healthy practices:* The strain of living in the modern world, with its sedentary and caloric lifestyle, can overload the natural healing systems of the body and produce sickness. Health practices, such as exercise, proper rest, living a balanced life, eating and drinking in moderation, and a

regular schedule, create a potent preventative regime that can go a long way toward slowing the aging process on all levels: body, mind, and spirit.

Value Aging As God's Gift

Retirement calls us to many things, not the least of which is to look closely at ourselves. As we accomplish this introspective task that aging offers, we come to more fully appreciate the greatness of God. We develop a grateful heart that views all of God's creation with heightened interest. Aging quickens our heart and nudges us closer to our true reality of Christ's presence within.

No one wants to grow old, certainly not the old that becomes a dispirited heart, a despondent soul, a tired body, and an unenlightened mind. Yet the diminishments of aging are real; they do inject themselves into the drama of our lives. We are called not to conquer aging, not to deny it, not even to overcome it. Rather, we are called to listen deeply to the life curriculum that aging offers and to appreciate the lessons inherent in it. Here is a large challenge of retirement: coming to a wiser appreciation, a humble gratitude, and a gracious understanding of life as never before.

Gratitude vs. Blaming

Gratitude is the power that sustains us through our entire maturation process, especially in our later years. Gratitude is profound thankfulness, a recognition of the giftedness in which we live, and an appreciation that everything is our teacher. Gratitude is adoration of God coupled with a sense of sanctified obligation. The opposite of gratitude is blaming.

When we blame we cut ourselves off from the healing power of God. Blaming is judgmental, reproachful, and critical. Blaming renders us caustic, rash, and acerbic. Blaming contorts our vision of ourselves, of others, and of God.

NOTE: For more on the topic of vital aging read: *The Twelve Keys to Spiritual Vitality: Powerful Lessons in Living Agelessly* by Dr. Johnson, published by Liguori Publications, 1998.

Affirmation

Lord, help me transform my attitudes about aging. I need to see the process of aging as part of your plan for me and for all humankind. Even though aging seems cruel and unnecessary to me at times, I know deep in my heart that it's really our gift to You. Aging is blessed! Help me to gradually become an "elder," a person who can show wisdom, peace, and quiet joy; a person who can offer counsel and sound guidance. Help me realize the vast difference between growing older and becoming "old." Help me resolve old conflicts, offer myself to others, develop a grateful heart, laugh at myself, continue to learn, and engage in healthy practices so that I can remain as open as possible to Your healing and illuminating touch all the days of my life.

CHAPTER 15

Get Going

*We are charged in retirement,
no less than when we were actively working full time,
to maximize our gifts by offering them to God's people.*

R. P. JOHNSON

Retirement Success Pearl #15

Stewardship and Service: The degree to which you can get going and offer your personal resources—your time, talents, and wealth—in God's service.

Retirement Challenge #15: How can I find spiritual replacements for the benefits I formerly received from my work?

The Need to Get Going: George's Revitalization

George opened his eyes as if he was awakening from the dead. He tried to turn his head as he lay in the coronary-care unit of University Hospital. The tubes, lines, and drips that extended from him, as though he was the center of some intricately spun medical spider web, constricted him to only the most minute movements. George's thoughts were muddy; his emotions were flat, but deep within him he felt a knot of fear. Although George mentally strained to find some point of orientation that was familiar, he could just peer at the clock at his bedside and see that it was 3:27 A.M. Once he realized where he was, it all cascaded down on him like an avalanche: his chest pain at work, calling his doctor, the trip to the emergency room, and the terse announcement from a doctor. "George," he recalled hearing, "you're going to have heart surgery."

George soon discovered the extent of his surgery: a five-way bypass that saved his life. Although George wasn't ready to retire—he was fifty-nine years old—his boss visited him when he returned home from the hospital and outlined a retirement plan that he felt more or less obliged to accept. Big changes for George! Within the space of two weeks his entire definition of himself changed: new body and no more work.

George considered his next life steps. First, there was extensive rehabilitation, but then what? George rather enjoyed the rehab schedule; he actually felt free, like he had a purpose and direction. When he no longer needed to go to the rehab center, George felt a shudder of fear. What would he do next?

George had been a real "company man." His thoughts were always with the company, his job, and how he could do things better. He worried about being the best he could be. He was pushed by some innate force that would ratchet him to ever higher levels of performance. His work was his world. George was the race horse; his work was his track. Without a track, however, where and how could he run? The question consumed him. From deep within, George felt surges of emptiness that swelled his desire to do something. George yearned to find a new venue where he could exercise his uniqueness. He wasn't content with an idle retirement. Although he knew that he couldn't work a "regular" job, he was certain there was a place, a setting, a situation, that would allow him to stretch as he had always done.

George eventually found that special place where he could be himself again, but not without traveling a rocky road that challenged places within himself that he never realized existed. George, like most of us, needed to experience the challenges of his new life before he could surmount the emptiness that was about to overtake him. Through this turmoil George realized that his work had meant so much more to him than a paycheck; it was his life. He recognized that he had always overdefined work, allowing it to control him. His intense personal investment in his work was probably one of the major factors that brought about his heart disease. How strange that the very issue he worshiped became the vehicle of his demise. Yet, from the ashes of his former life structure, George did eventually learn that he needed to fulfill some of the "basics" of working, even as a retired person.

Five Benefits of Working

Like George, many of us let our work become our way of life. We let it pervade our thinking and form the basis of our assumptions. We turn to our work to give us a way of perceiving ourselves and others; our work becomes our identity. Our work defines us, causes our emotions to rise and fall, and becomes the basis of many of our life decisions. Beginning at an early age, we heard our parents and friends ask, "So what do you want to be when you grow up?" That simple question taught us that work would give foundation, structure, and direction to our lives. Gradually, our work becomes who we are.

Like George, most of us work for the greater part of our life. Work gives us benefits that have become so embedded in us that they have raised themselves to the level of "need." A need is something that we must satisfy; otherwise, we begin to lose ourselves and ultimately get sick in some way. These needs that we have developed during our working years are among the deepest and strongest in our entire being—and they do not evaporate when we retire. These needs have been imprinted into our sinew; they are part of us. Retiring from our full-time, paid, active work life does not wash away these needs. The personal benefits we derive from working remain well entrenched within us; they seek expression in our postretirement years as they did in our pre-retirement years. Here is the crux of this fifteenth retirement success factor: finding the means and personal direction to arrange our retirement years so that we can continue to satisfy these work-related benefits and needs.

Generally, our work provides us with five benefits that provide us with an overall level of life satisfaction. When George was abruptly disconnected from his work, he was also severed from fulfilling several of these key personal benefits that had become specific personal needs. Until he was able to find replacements for them these needs snapped at George every day of his imposed retirement.

1. *Financial remuneration:* Even though we may not have received tremendous financial rewards from our work, we did receive a remuneration that enabled us to meet our material needs. Usually this remuneration takes the form of a paycheck. Many of us look to this benefit of work as the single focus for our replacement efforts as we prepare for retirement; we look only to replace our income. Sadly, this myopia may blind us to the fact that there are four other benefit/needs that we must somehow satisfy in retirement.

2. *Time management:* Our work gives our life structure; it man-

ages our time. Some would say that our work overmanages our time, or even commands our time. The fact remains that our work usually lets us know what we will be doing come Monday morning. The time management function, or benefit of our work, keeps our life orderly and "in-sync" with the beat of the culture. It keeps us "in the loop," in the mainstream of life.

3. *Sense of utility:* Having personal utility, a sense that what we do is worthy and helpful to others, injects a feeling of meaning into life. Our life has implicit meaning through our work by assisting God's people in some way. We benefit God's children in some way through our work by bringing or serving peace and justice. Our work gives us a "cause" from which we derive a qualitative measure of satisfaction.

4. *Status:* It is from our work, our role in society, that we accrue a certain status. We have a definite place in the scheme of the world. Having a social role is necessary for everyone, because it gives status. Status is that combined sense of personal worth and identity that we derive from knowing who and what we are.

5. *Socialization:* Our work brings us in close—if not constant—contact with many of God's people. We interact with them. We actually become connected with some in a deeply sharing manner. At our work we develop relationships, form friendships, and learn how to cooperate at higher and higher levels as the projects we and our organization conceive demand more and more interaction.

These five benefits become a part of us to such a degree that we cannot simply discard them without some emotional, psychological, and spiritual consequences. How many times have we known of persons, who were formerly involved with their work, emotionally "crash" sometime after their retirement. Usually it's not because of some sudden catastrophic event like running out of money or losing their home. Normally, it's a slow wearing away of the individual; it's the unseen losses that gradually push them out of balance, to the brink of personal fragmentation that can sometimes escalate into despair if left unaddressed. One or more of these five may be at the heart of their brokenness.

Service and Stewardship

Whether we work for our paycheck or collect a pension makes little difference to God. As God's children, we are expected to continue our search for God in all that we do. We are charged in retirement, no less than when we were actively working full time, to maximize our gifts by offering them to God's people. As we saw in Chapter 8, there is no shortage of problems in our world, nor is there any lack of talent. We possess the talent, our gifts are from God, and so they are really God's gifts; we have no right to restrict God's gifts from God's children. The urges that George felt deep within his soul were urges from God within nudging him to find places, people, situations, and occasions where he could utilize his gifts—God's gifts. This is real stewardship, utilizing our talents in ways that God intended. We're not called to light the entire world, just to light our little corner of it.

This fifteenth retirement success factor invites us to discover ways of replacing the five benefits we formerly derived from working. Such an accomplishment is not a luxury; rather it's a necessity. Just as we need water and food to live, we need to fulfill these five benefits/needs of working throughout our entire lives. One of the ways we can do this is to develop a personal ministry.

A ministry is a job that we do not for money, not for personal fame, not because someone asked us; rather, we develop a ministry because God needs this job accomplished. A job is for us, whereas a ministry is for God. Retirement affords us the marvelous opportunity of pursuing a ministry, perhaps for the first time in our lives. Life problems are everywhere; just read the morning paper and we can discover hundreds. Right there in those pages—pages we've read for years—we will find ministry situations, opportunities for offering service to God's people while being a good steward of our own gifts and talents. Read the paper with new eyes; read as Jesus would read. See the human suffering and recognize the many opportunities for demonstrating our most potent power: love!

A ministry of service and stewardship is waiting for you. This ministry will bring joy and personal fulfillment beyond what you thought possible. You can transform the needs you developed from working for so long into the very vehicles that can give you the staff of life: the knowledge that you are doing God's work in God's time. Once the first benefit/need of working, that of financial remuneration, is fulfilled, you become free to concentrate on the other four. Sadly, all too many retirees end their search for happiness when they know their wallets will be sufficiently stocked. All too few look beyond the financial need to the other four needs. They "take the fake" of the world by presuming that the purpose of retirement is to find ever greater amounts of fun and rest. They unknowingly, yet quite completely, overlook their more personal needs, their psychological needs. All four needs beyond finances—time management, utility, socialization, and status—can be wonderfully fulfilled in ministry. Indeed ministry brings yet another fulfillment, greater perhaps than the rest: that of knowing you are on God's road, knowing you have dedicated yourself to God's work, and finding real peace, genuine happiness, and lasting well being like you have never known before.

Making a commitment to a ministry, developing a life cause, does not mean that you need to dedicate every waking moment to solving the problems of this world. Jesus said that the poor would always be with us. To me this means that because this is the world, there will always be problems. Our goal is not to become the world's "fixer"; rather, our goal is to shed the light of Christ in one dark corner that we have discovered. When we shine our own light, we are shining God's light there, and in the process we discover who we really are.

God is purposeful, and retirement has purpose. Its purpose is a continuation of the purpose we have had all through the years. The purpose of retirement is to extend our learning how to love. Each day of our life we are called to learn how to love better. Retirement ushers in a new curriculum of love, teaching new ways of loving.

Each day of your retirement ask yourself: "How and where can I learn to love better today?" The answers you discover will propel you on a daily adventure, an adventure of cosmic proportion, a thrilling adventure of delight, of awe, and of peace. These are the gifts that the challenges of retirement offer to you.

Charity vs. Judgment

The power that can energize us to meet the challenge of this fifteenth retirement challenge is charity. Charity is recognizing the needs of another and working to help others in a selfless manner. Charity is bighearted; it expects nothing in return. The opposite of charity is judgment. This is not the wise judgment that we may think of as a part of maturation; this judgment is the kind that causes us to judge, to become judgmental, to criticize, offend, and belittle.

Affirmation

I know Lord that I have received many benefits from my years of working. I have defined myself more or less by my work over the years. Today I have arrived at a juncture where I must re-define myself. I can no longer use my work as my personal definition, I need to construct new replacements for the needs that I developed in the past and which are still requirements of my being. I know that my gifts are really Your gifts to the world and to your children. I am called to bring these gifts to the table of human activity in ways that are different from the ways I formerly offered my gifts when I was employed full time. This transition is not an easy one, and yet I know that You, dear Lord knock at the door to my heart requesting that I respond to Your call. I can meet this challenge by discovering my unique ministry. In the process find yet another piece of the true happiness that You wish for me.

Epilogue

One of the goals of my ministry is to train "retirement coaches" for each and every parish and congregation. This person, couple, or group serves as a resource for helping those preparing for a new retirement, one that is a spiritual journey, as well as those who are already retired, to make the most of their retirement years. The JOHNSON Institute offers a training course, in either a two-day or a self-study format, that awards certification in this vital ministry. The course teaches all that is necessary to develop a retirement ministry in any Christian church, a ministry that can be used as a springboard for so many other maturing-adult faith formation ministries. For more information, contact:

The JOHNSON Institute
1714 Big Horn Basin, Suite 400
Wildwood (St. Louis), MO 63011-4819
Web site: SeniorAdultMinistry.com
Phone: 636-273-6898
Fax: 636-273-6899
Email: drjohnson@lifelongadultministry.org

Putting It All Together

The following exercises allow you to personalize and extend the information for each of the fifteen retirement success "pearls" described in the preceding chapters. These can serve as your own personal workbook, or they can be used when presenting this material in a group format. Either way, they can assist you in grasping the essence of retirement preparation and planning in a robust and comprehensive way.

1. Career Reorientation

Each of us has been "endowed" with varying levels of a "work ethic," the need to do well in our work so we can feel a positive sense of fulfillment. This concept is also called "identification with work." Those with a high "identification" register a strong need to excel at their career in order to feel good about who and what they are. Others with low work identification draw their self-esteem from activities or relationships outside of work.

DIRECTIONS: Respond to the following questions. Put as much personal data as possible into your responses.

1. How high is your "work ethic" on a scale of 1–10, with 1 being a very low work ethic and with 10 being a very high work ethic?

2. How did you develop the work ethic you possess?

3. Who were the persons who contributed the most to the development of your particular work ethic? Describe their input.

4. How has your work ethic contributed positively to your overall personal development? How has it taken from you?

2. Retirement Value

The very definition of retirement has changed dramatically in the past decade. Retirement is no longer conceived of as an end but rather as a new beginning. Retirement is seen as a vital and potential-packed transition moving us toward increased growth and development rather than away from life.

DIRECTIONS: In the spaces provided below, identify those things, that is, those events, relationships, activities, and so on, that you are moving away from as you approach (or experience) retirement, and those things you are moving (growing) toward.

As I approach my retirement stage of personal development, I will (am) move...

Away from...	...and move toward...
1.	1.
2.	2.
3.	3.
4.	4.
5.	5.
6.	6.

3. Personal Empowerment

No one is completely self-empowered or other-empowered; that would be impossible. Commonly, we are more self-empowered about some things and more other-empowered about others. Each of us lies somewhere along the spectrum of empowerment in the many tasks and roles that we perform in our total lives, sometimes edging closer to one end or the other. This factor of personal empowerment, although usually a rather stable personality trait, can become rather fluid, at times leaning us more toward self-empowerment, while at other times leaning us more away from self-empowerment and toward other-empowerment.

DIRECTIONS: Listed below are the six life arenas. Try to esti-mate the amount or level of self-empowerment you have in each of these six. Give at least one example of how you are self- or other-empowered in each of the six life arenas. (See Appendix Two for descriptions of each life arena.)

1. Career:

2. Family:

3. Relationships:

4. Self: (self-concept and body-concept):

5. Faith:

6. Leisure:

4. Physical Wellness

Your perception of your health status relates directly to your success in retirement. It is impossible to separate your mind from
your body or either from your spirit; they are all interconnected.
You are holistic; you are holy! If your mind tells you that you
are healthy and that you can influence the overall condition of
your body, the likelihood of this being true is infinitely great. If
your mind tells you that you are in poor health and sickly, the
probability of this being true is likewise increased.

DIRECTIONS: Write a paragraph or two on how your mind
and spirit assist you in your path toward wellness. Include in your
response the degree you believe in and participate in "alternative"
forms of healing, that is, nonmedical forms of healing.

5. Monetary Adequacy

Money is generally considered the keystone of retirement preparation. Unquestionably, financial security exerts a powerful direct and indirect influence on your retirement timing and your retirement lifestyle. However, money alone cannot "purchase" retirement success. Certainly, financial solvency can buffer any life transition and ease the sting of unfortunate events in your life. However, the importance of money can be overemphasized to the point where you come to unwisely believe that retirement preparation and financial sufficiency are synonymous.

DIRECTIONS: In the spaces provided below, identify three things that you are thankful for regarding your methods of handling finances, and three suggestions you might have for improving the way you handle your fiances.

The three things I am thankful for in regard to the way I handle my finances are

1.

2.

3.

The three suggestions I would like to make regarding the way I handle my finances are

1.

2.

3.

6. Quality of Life—Present

Knowing that your current life satisfaction is rooted in the quality of how you traversed your previous life stages is central to your temporal happiness. Having this perspective on your life stages is directly connected with your understanding of factor six: quality of life—present. To gain excellence in this factor you must have successfully mastered the specific challenges presented to you in the preceding life stages; otherwise, you may feel conflicted and unable to enjoy fully a high degree of life satisfaction. You can easily become overwhelmed with unresolved issues from previous life stages that were never resolved or mastered.

DIRECTIONS: In each of the six life arenas listed below, identify any unfinished or unresolved issues that make themselves known to you from time to time. These could be anything that fits in the categories of "I wish I had...," "I wish I could have been...,"I wish this didn't happen...," and so on.

1. Career/Ministry/Life Cause:

2. Family:

3. Relationships:

4. Self (self-concept and body-concept):

5. Faith:

6. Leisure:

7. Quality of Life—Future

In order for you to be successful at anything, you require motivation. There are two broad types of motivation: (1) positive motivation, defined as the tendency to achieve success; and (2) negative motivation, the tendency to avoid failure. Rarely can you identify tasks which are clearly either all positively or all negatively motivated. Usually there are elements of both present: creating an internal struggle with every task attempted. There are some who believe that as we mature, each of us tends to gradually change our motivation away from positive motivation and toward negative motivation. If this is true, then one's future quality of life seems to be motivated by avoiding failure, meaning we will probably not take risks as readily as we did in our younger years.

DIRECTIONS: In the space provided below, identify the risks and the motivations that you undertook in your younger years, as well as any that you project you will be taking in the future.

AGE	RISK	MOTIVATION (+ or -)
1 – 10		
11 – 20		
21 – 30		

AGE	RISK	MOTIVATION (+ or -)
31 – 40		
41 – 50		
51 – 60		
61 – 70		
71 – 80		
81 – 90		
91+		

8. Spirituality/Meaning
Spiritual Life Questionnaire

DIRECTIONS: Read the five statements below and rate each of them as to what best describes your thoughts and feelings right now. Total up your score, using the scale given.

1. I'm satisfied with how I feel God's support and assistance when I need help with something that might be troubling me.

   Almost always_____ Some of the time____Hardly ever_____
2. I'm satisfied with the way I can discuss (pray) items of personal interest with God and share problems with God.

   Almost always_____ Some of the time____Hardly ever_____
3. I'm satisfied with how I see God as understanding my needs so I can healthfully grow, personally develop, and spiritually mature in my personal faith life.

   Almost always_____ Some of the time____Hardly ever_____
4. I'm satisfied how I can express my feelings to God and that God understands and accepts my emotions for what they are.

   Almost always_____ Some of the time____Hardly ever_____
5. I'm satisfied with the quality of the time I share together with God.

   Almost always_____ Some of the time____Hardly ever_____

Scoring:
1. Give yourself 2 points for every "Almost always" response

   _ _ _ _ _
2. Give yourself 1 point for every "Some of the time" response

   _ _ _ _ _
3. You get no points for "Hardly ever" response   _ _ _ _ _

   Total Score _ _ _ _ _

Compare your score with others. There is no average score; everyone is different.

9. Respect for Leisure

One of the ways we can best motivate ourselves toward a more constructive leisure arena in retirement (or approaching it) is to answer some focused questions pertaining to our current leisure life.

DIRECTIONS: Below are questions that pertain to your leisure arena. Respond to the questions with as much detail as you can.

1. What courses or classes have you taken to enhance your participation in your leisure arena? Describe.

2. What risks, if any, have you taken in your leisure arena? Describe.

3. To what degree do you feel creative in your leisure life arena? Describe.

4. What kind of leisure traveling have you done in the last decade? Describe.

5. What were your favorite movies, radio, and/or television programs during the last decade of your life? Describe.

6. What would you say is the highlight of your leisure life arena right now? In the past? Explain.

7. Who is your favorite leisure time companion?

8. How has your leisure life arena changed over the years?

9. What level of meaning, personal satisfaction, and joy do you derive from your leisure life arena? Describe.

10. To what degree have you fulfilled your leisure "dreams"?

10. Personal Flexibility

Change has been called the "watchword of the universe" in that the only thing that doesn't change in the universe is the fact that everything is always changing. Change, then, is something we are constantly called to do on a daily basis; without changing we would soon get sick. How well do you handle change? What forces stop you from undertaking the changes that you want to make in your life (personal change blockers), and what forces motivate you to incorporate change into your life (personal change enhancers)? The answer to these questions are an indication of your overall emotional health at this time.

DIRECTIONS: Below are listed the six life arenas. Next to each you will find two columns, one marked "Blockers," and the other marked "Enhancers." Next to each life arena list only one change, however small, that you *would like to make* in this arena of your life. Next to the change list any of the "blockers" and/or "enhancers" that may be operative right now in your life.

Arena	Blockers	Enhancers

1. Career/Ministry/Life Cause:

2. Family:

Arena	Blockers	Enhancers

3. Relationships:

4. Self:

5. Faith:

6. Leisure:

11. Spiritual Luster

We are called to live in the "now," in fact, the only time you can live your life is in the present. As Dr. Wayne Dyer likes to say, "Yesterday is only a canceled check and tomorrow is promised to no one...you only have today." As Christians, too, we are called to love. When can you love but right now; you can't love yesterday, nor can you love tomorrow. Today is the day for action, the day for doing, the time to live and love. Often, however, we get stuck in thoughts of the "guilty past" or the "fearful future." How much of your own internal thoughts are tied up in thinking about these two areas—the past or the future?

DIRECTIONS: Listed below are the six life arenas (again). Next to each are three columns, the first is marked "Past," the second is marked "Now," and the third is marked "Future." Guesstimate what percentage of your thoughts in each of the life arenas is focused on: past, present, or future. Remember the three must total 100 percent.

Arena	Past	Present	Future
1. Career:			
2. Family:			
3. Relationships:			
4. Self:			
5. Faith:			
6. Leisure:			

12. Caregiving Responsibilities

DIRECTIONS: Answer each of the following 20 questions on a scale of 1 to 10. A response of 1 indicates that this statement does not describe your thinking at all, while a response of 10 indicates that this statement describes your thinking perfectly. Try to be as accurate as you can in your responses between 1 and 10.

_____ 1. Aging is not good. It brings loss, dependency, non-productivity, withdrawal, and decay.

_____ 2. Aging is a developmental challenge designed by God so we can learn better who we truly are.

_____ 3. Aging brings an end to emotional growth and personal development.

_____ 4. Growth and development of one's interior life over the entire life span gives purpose and meaning to all of life.

_____ 5. Aging takes the people I love away from me.

_____ 6. Aging gives life; it moves one toward the ultimate transition to eternal life.

_____ 7. I need to be the perfect friend and caregiver to all elders.

_____ 8. I am the person who I am; I have no need to portray myself as anything other than what I am.

_____ 9. My relationship with my elders needs to be unchangeable; it needs to remain what it always has been.

_____ 10. I am open to God's healing power in my relationship with all my elders.

_____ 11. I need to "do it all" for my elders. I must protect them.

_____ 12. My goal is to "be with" my elders, not be continuously "doing for" them.

_____ 13. My elders needs come before any of my own.

_____ 14. I will love and honor my elders as I do my family and all other members of my religious community.

____ 15. My relationship with my elders can and should be great.

____ 16. I cannot force a particular type of relationship with my elders. I will strive to be myself with them.

____ 17. My elders must be right (even if they do seem illogical).

____ 18. My elders are fallible: saying "no" to them is necessary at times in order to sustain an "adult-adult" relationship.

____ 19. I need always be in control with my elders.

____ 20. God is always in charge.

Scoring: 1. Total up your scores for the odd-numbered statements. 2. Total up your scores for the even-numbered statements. Which is bigger? If the total you scored for the odd-numbered statements is higher than the total for the even-numbered statements, you may need to change your attitudes about caregiving.

13. Home Life

Home life can be a marvelous and enriching component of life or it can be, on the contrary, the most hurtful and resistive way of living there could be. Expectations are usually high for the kind of living we do in our own home, but many times these expectations are not fulfilled, leaving us with a sense of emptiness and alienation. How do you see your home life?

DIRECTIONS: Respond to the following five questions, using your home as your reference point. If you live alone, then use the closest "family" to you as your reference. Try to use the people with whom you live as your reference point.

Family Questionnaire

To what degree (1–10) are you satisfied...

_____ 1. that you can turn to your family for help?

_____ 2. with the way your family talks over things with you and shares problems with you?

_____ 3. that your family accepts and supports your wishes?

_____ 4. with the way your family expresses affection and responds to your emotions, such as anger, sorrow, or love?

_____ 5. with the way your family and you share time together?

Scoring: Add up your five response scores into a total score. Multiply this total score by two. You have now produced your family-life score. If you are in a group, compare your scores with other group members.

14. Maturation Vitality

My work convinces me that people who feel youthful and have high energy levels are the ones who have the greatest opportunities to achieve overall success in retirement and in their later years in general.

DIRECTIONS: To what degree do the following twelve functions relate to your aging? Respond to each statement on a scale of 1 to 10, with 1 meaning that this does not describe you and 10 indicating that this very closely describes you.

_____ 1. I am transforming my attitudes about aging to resemble the statement, "One must be very mature in order to be youthful."

_____ 2. I seek love everywhere I look.

_____ 3. I delight in connecting with others and in sharing deeply.

_____ 4. I live in the present moment, in the "now."

_____ 5. I accept my true self, my holy self.

_____ 6. I forgive others and myself.

_____ 7. I let go of anger and other inner turmoil.

_____ 8. I regularly give of myself to others.

_____ 9. I routinely celebrate my faith.

_____ 10. I am actively in the process of discovering the deep meaning in life.

_____ 11. I make my feelings work for me.

_____ 12. I achieve a harmonious balance in my life.

Scoring: There are no formal scores here—the higher your score the more you are "on track" to discovering the best from your own maturational path.

15. Stewardship and Service

Some people seem to forget that the retirement stage of living (however you conceive of it to be for you) has or will emerge from the foundation of life experience they have built all through their previous years. However they choose to develop and manage this segment of their life differently from former stages in their life, it is nonetheless a continuation of their life. They are still the same person they have been all along, with the same personality they had all through the years. They may have a new lifestyle in retirement, but it's still the same person!

DIRECTIONS: Below are listed the six rewards or benefits that you receive(d) from your work. Next to each estimate mark the degree (1–10) to which this reward or benefit is (was) valuable for you. Then write a short statement about why you evaluated this work benefit the way you did and how you believe this might (has) change in retirement.

_____ 1. Mission of your faith:

_____ 2. Just remuneration:

____ 3. Time management:

____ 4. Sense of utility:

____ 5. Status:

____ 6. Socialization:

APPENDIX 2

Generating Retirement Options

In Chapter 6, the notion of the six life arenas was introduced. Everything that you do in your life can be grouped into one or more of these six arenas. Actually most of us are "doing things" in each life arena simultaneously. Indeed, your life can be likened to a six-ring circus, which has six different acts going on in each ring of the circus at the same time. Even though all six acts are happening at the same time, we can only focus on one at a time. The importance of the six arenas for us as we look at retirement is that together they form a framework upon which you can "hang" various "options" for your retirement success.

Under each of the descriptions of the six life arenas you see general categories of potential activities for your retirement. You can identify the specific categories under each life arena that best meet your needs, from these you can then develop your own more targeted retirement options which you can then further investigate.

Six Life Arenas

1. *Career or Work Life Arena:* This arena encompasses your work and day-to-day activities in life. It includes everything you do, think about, plan for and worry about that is somehow connected to your work. If you are already retired, you may think that you don't have any work, but this is not true. Everyone needs a "life cause," something that occupies their need for usefulness, something that helps others, something that brings comfort, or in some way, however small, serves to forward the ongoing growth and development of the community. Even if you are not performing paid work any longer you still "work," you still are pursuing a "life's dream," a "mission," or a compelling passion. All of this is considered part of the career or work life arena.

Consider which of the following general categories seem most appropriate for your life right now. Following this, identify specific activities under that general category which could become retirement options and where you may find fulfillment and satisfaction.

new job
time management
continue current employment
income management
part-time work
pursuing the career "dream"
volunteer community service
retraining
other vocational options
consultant
search for status
self-employment

pursuing your "dream"
developing a "life cause"
having a "life purpose"

2. *Family Life Arena:* Families are with us forever. We begin our life journey in a family and we usually leave this life from the midst of a family. During the journey, we perform many roles, from infant, to adolescent, to young adult, adult, and elder. Along the way we are daughters or sons, parents, aunts or uncles, grandparents, and so on. We learn our traditions, establish our identities, and develop our values from our family experiences. These continuously influence us throughout our whole life. Our loved ones mean so much to us, and in retirement this meaning generally increases.

Scan the categories of family living, and identify the ones which offer "options" for you both now and in the future.

Respect and appreciate uniqueness of family
travel
marriage (intimate) strengths
intimacy development
household maintenance
common adventures
caregiving
money management
genealogy/extended family
communication enhancement
traditions maintenance
lifestyle management
shared fun

3. *Relationships Life Arena:* We have many different relationships with many different people, each involves us in varying
levels of sharing. Our relationship with our auto mechanic for
example is identifiably different from our relationship with
our spouse. Intimacy emerges in a relationship when we take
the risk of sharing ourselves deeply. Those relationships we
value the most usually receive our deeper sharing of thoughts,
feelings, commitments, and time. Our ability to make and keep
friends is seen as a primary competency for finding fulfillment
in life. We need people in our lives.

Identify those areas where you believe you can enhance your relationship life arena and provide retirement options for yourself.

    church
    athletic or other competitive teams
    social contact organizations
    friends
    socialization
    shared experiences
    clubs
    confidante
    community projects

4. *Self Life Arena:* This is the intrapersonal arena of your life. It
is in the life arena where you relate to your inner self—your
values, beliefs, perceptions, thoughts, feelings, and decisions.
This arena actually has two distinct components. The first is
our internal relationship with our self. This includes such issues as self-esteem, feelings about ourselves, self-confidence,
self-control, self-discipline, and self-regard. While each of
these overlaps a bit, they all speak to an internal sense of self-
understanding. The second part of the selflife arena is your
relationship with your own body. What is your body image?

Once again, identify those general categories where you would like to inject greater "zest" into your life, and then identify several specific actions or activities that you could pursue in each and provide retirement options for you.

self-improvement activities
school
self-appreciation
self-exploration
health and wellness
dynamic self-understanding
modify self-definition
physical shape improvement
health maintenance
mental-health promotion
self-study

5. *Faith Life or Spiritual Life Arena:* As we mature there is a progressive and normal desire to find spiritual comfort and deeper meaning in our lives; we long for an open and personal relationship with God. For some people, this means greater involvement in church and religious activities. Here we can refine our values and a belief system in ways which moves us forward with renewed hope and spiritual integrity. In this life arena we identify a deeper purpose in life which gives us connection with the Divine.

Here are some general suggestions for enriching your spiritual life arena; from these you can develop specific "options" for retirement growth and personal development.

missionary work
theology study
evangelizing

discern spiritual calling
participate in faith organizations
life meaning clarification
spiritual study groups
prayer and contemplation
good works

6. *Leisure Life Arena:* This arena was thoroughly defined and
   discussed in Chapter 9; you might want to review the themes
   that emerged from this chapter for you.

Here again are the general categories for the arena from which
you can generate specific retirement options best suited for your
personality and your overall life situation.

spectator appreciation activities
creative expression activities
adopt leisure mentality
leisure interests exploration
solitary relaxation activities
physical exercise activities
intellectual stimulation activities
social interaction activities

My Action Plan for Success in Retirement

Now that you have (1) learned about each of the fifteen "pearls" for retirement success, (2) completed an exercise for each one designed to extend and personalize that "pearl" for you, and (3) surveyed various activities in each of your six life arenas, discovering specific options for your growth and development. It's now time to compact all this information into a usable action plan for your retirement living.

I recommend that your action be short and crisp rather than lengthy and cumbersome. Therefore, I'd like to suggest that you identify only three goals for your personal retirement success in the next year. Even if you're more than a year from retirement, or if you're already retired, you still need goals for successful action. I find that more than three goals per year only become confusing and substantially raises the likelihood that your goals will remain unfulfilled. Under each of your three goals, list at least two specific objectives that you will need to accomplish in order to complete the goal. This action plan is simple, yet it is powerful.

I. Retirement goal #1:

_____

_____

    A. Objective 1:

_____

_____

_____

B. Objective 2:

_____

_____

_____

II. Retirement goal #2:

_____

_____

_____

A. Objective 1:

_____

_____

_____

B. Objective 2:

_____

_____

_____

III. Retirement goal #3:

_____

_____

    A. Objective 1:

_____

_____

_____

    B. Objective 2:

_____

_____

_____

Bibliography

Chapter 1

Helmstetter, Shad. *You Can Excel in Times of Change.* New York: Pocket Books, 1991.

Whitehead, Evelyn E., and James D. Whitehead. *Christian Life Patterns.* New York: Crossroad, 1993.

Rupp, Joyce, OSM. *Praying Our Goodbyes.* South Bend, IN: Ave Maria Press, 1988.

Chapter 2

Rohr, Richard. *A Spirituality of Subtraction,* Cincinnati, OH: St. Anthony Messenger Press, 1987.

Bianchi, Eugene, Ph.D. *Aging With Grace.* Cincinnati, OH: St. Anthony Messenger Press, 1993.

Van Hoose, William H., and Maureen R. Worth. "Work and Leisure," in *Adulthood in the Life Cycle.* Dubuque, IA: Brown, 1982.

Chapter 3

Dyer, Wayne W. *Everyday Wisdom.* Carson, CA: Hay House, 1993.

Kalellis, Peter M. *Pick Up Your Couch and Walk,* New York: Crossroad, 1994.

Powell, John, S.J. *Happiness Is an Inside Job.* Dallas, TX: Tabor Publishing, 1989.

May, Gerald. *Simply Sane.* New York: Crossroad, 1993.

Chapter 4

Bakken, Kenneth L. *The Call to Wholeness.* New York: Crossroad, 1992.

Bakken, Kenneth L. and Kathleen Hoffler. *The Journey Toward Wholeness.* New York: Crossroad, 1992.

Chopra, Deepak, M.D. *Ageless Body, Timeless Mind.* New York: Harmony Press, 1993.

Johnson, Richard P. *Body, Mind, Spirit: Tapping the Healing Power Within.* Liguori, MO: Liguori Publications, 1992.

Moyers, Bill. *Healing the Mind.* New York: Doubleday, 1993.

Spencer, Sabina A., and John D. Adams. *Life Choices: Growing Through Personal Transitions.* San Luis Obispo, CA: Impact Publishers, 1990.

Chapter 5

Albom, Mitch. *Tuesdays With Morrie.* New York: Bantam Books, 1997.

Haughey, John C. *The Holy Use of Money.* New York: Crossroad, 1992.

Martindale, Judith and Mary J. Moses. *Creating Your Own Future.* Naperville, IL: Sourcebooks Trade, 1991.

Chapter 6

Peck, M. Scott. *A Road Less Traveled.* New York: Touchstone, Simon & Schuster, 1978.

Quoist, Michael. *New Prayers.* New York: Crossroad, 1993.

Finley, Mitch. *Everybody Has a Guardian Angel.* New York: Crossroad, 1994.

Livingston, Patricia H. *Lessons of the Heart.* South Bend, IN: Ave Maria Press, 1992.

Chapter 7

Cousins, Norman. *Head First: The Biology of Hope and the Healing Power of the Human Spirit.* New York: Penguin Books, 1989.

Fiand, Barbara. *Embraced by Compassion.* New York: Crossroad, 1993.

Sinclair, Carole. *When Women Retire: The Problems They Face and How to Solve Them.* New York: Crown Publishers, 1992.

Chapter 8

Frankl, Viktor E. *The Unheard Cry for Meaning.* New York: Simon & Schuster, 1978.

Carmody, John. *Cancer and Faith.* Mystic, CT: Twenty-Third Publications, 1994.

Lonsdale, David. *Listening to the Music of the Spirit.* South Bend, IN: Ave Maria Press, 1992.

Sofield, Loughlan. *Self-Esteem and Christian Growth.* South Bend, IN: Ave Maria Press, 1992.

Sinetar, Marsha. *Elegant Choices, Healing Choices.* Mahwah, NJ: Paulist Press, 1988.

Chapter 9

Doohan, Leonard. *Leisure: A Spiritual Need.* South Bend, IN: Ave Maria Press, 1990.

Minnihan, Joanne. *Leisure Is Where You Find It,* audiotape presentation, AGES, Inc., St. Louis, MO, 1988.

Neulinger, J. *The Psychology of Leisure.* Springfield, IL: Charles C. Thomas, 1976.

Riker, Harold. "Potential Crisis Situations for Older Persons: Preretirement, Retirement, Leisure, Relocation, Housing" in Ganikos, Mary (ed.) *Counseling the Aged.* Washington, DC: American Personnel and Guidance Association, 1979.

Swenson, Harriet K. *Visible and Vital.* Mahwah, NJ: Paulist Press, 1994.

Chapter 10

Nouwen, Henri. *Beyond the Mirror.* New York: Crossroad, 1992.

Clark, Keith, O.F.M. Cap. *The Skilled Participant.* South Bend, IN: Ave Maria Press, 1988.

Ripple, Paula. *Growing Strong at Broken Places.* South Bend, IN: Ave Maria Press, 1986.

McCullum, Eric C. "Making Change," Vol. 31, in *New Choices for the Best Years,* pp. 86–89, Nov. 1991.

Siligman, Martin E. P. *Learned Optimism.* New York: Alfred A. Knopf, 1991.

Toffler, Alvin. *Future Shock.* New York: Random House, 1970.

Chapter 11

Burt, Donald X. *But When You Are Old.* Collegeville, MN: The Liturgical
    Press, 1992.
May, Gerald. *Simply Sane.* New York: Crossroad Publications, 1993.
Carroll, Patrick, S.J., and Katherine M. Dyckman, SNJM. *Chaos or Creation.*
    Mahwah, NJ: Paulist Press, 1986.

Chapter 12

Johnson, Richard P. *How to Honor Your Aging Parents: Fundamental Prin-
    ciples of Caregiving.* Liguori, MO: Liguori Lifespan, 1999.
Hover, Margaret. *Caring for Yourself When Caring for Others.* Mystic, CT:
    Twenty-Third Publications, 1994.
Nouwen, Henri J. *The Lonely Search for God.* South Bend, IN: Ave Maria
    Press, 1989.

Chapter 13

Moore, Thomas. *Care of the Soul.* New York: Harper Collins, 1992.
Westley, Dick. *Redemptive Intimacy: A New Perspective for the Journey to
    Adult Faith.* Mystic, CT: Twenty-Third Publications, 1981.
Sofield, Laughlan, ST, Carroll Juliano, SHCJ, and Rosine Hammett, CSC.
    Design for Wholeness. South Bend, IN: Ave Maria Press, 1990.

Chapter 14

Johnson, Richard P. *The 12 Keys to Spiritual Vitality: Powerful Lessons on
    Living Agelessly,* Liguori, MO: Liguori Publications, 1998.
Burt, Donald X. *But When You Are Older.* Collegeville, MN: Liturgical
    Press, 1992.
Bianchi, Eugene C. *Aging As a Spiritual Journey.* New York: Crossroad,
    1993.
Reilly, Maria, S.P. *Now That I Am Old.* Mystic, CT: Twenty-Third Publica-
    tions, 1994.

Chapter 15

Shaffer, Robert W. *Occupying the Summit.* Plano, TX: Wordware Publish-
    ing, 1989.
Cort-Van Arsdale, Diana and Phyllis Newman. *Transitions: A Woman's Guide
    to Successful Retirement.* New York: Harper Collins, 1991.
Lee, Fred and Alice Lee. *A Field Guide to Retirement.* New York: Doubleday,
    1991.

Index

About the Author

Richard P. Johnson holds a doctorate in gerontological counseling. He has worked extensively with religious groups across the United States and Canada, helping them to grow more vibrantly in the middle and later phases of their lives. He is the former director of Behavioral Sciences in the Department of Family Practice at St. John's Mercy Medical Center in St. Louis, Missouri. Currently, Dr. Johnson is executive director of the Association for Senior Adult Ministry, located in St. Louis. His books include *Body, Mind, Spirit: Tapping the Healing Power Within You; Caring for Your Aging Parents; and The Twelve Keys to Spiritual Vitality: Powerful Lessons on Living Agelessly.* He lives *in* Wildwood, Missouri.

Of Related Interest

All My Days
A Personal Life Review

What greater gift could there be for senior adults than delving into the special moments, memories, and traditions that have shaped and enriched their lives? This personal journal provides a way for seniors to use their individuality and creativity in writing an account of their important and meaningful life events.

ISBN: 978-0-7648-0643-8

The 12 Keys to Spiritual Vitality
Powerful Lessons on Living Agelessly

Aging is not the beginning of the end, but is part of God's eternal plan for human happiness. Through this book, readers will tap into the wisdom and grace that come with aging and discover the keys to maturing in the way God intended.

ISBN: 978-0-7648-0230-0

Grounded in God
A Mature Experience of Faith

Grounded in God is a book of reflections dedicated to the growth of faith, hope, love, and laughter in the second half of life. It is a collection of 50 articles, which were selected from over 400 that the authors have published in Catholic newspaper columns throughout the country. The personal experiences shared here are down to earth and easy to read. Instead of focusing on the end of life, this book helps readers focus on living life to the end. Through ever-deepening faith, every day becomes an adventure.

ISBN: 978-0-7648-1408-2

To order visit your local bookstore or call 800-325-9521 or visit us at www.liguori.org